PRIVATE LANDSCAPES

PRIVATE LANDSCAPES

Creating Form, Vistas, and Mystery in the Garden

by Caroline Seebohm and Christopher Simon Sykes

Design by Laurence Vétu-Kane

Garden plans by Perry Guillot, Landscape Architect

CLARKSON N. POTTER, INC. / PUBLISHERS

FOR SOPHIE, HUGH, AND LILY

Flower-lined steps and paths at Garsington Manor, near Oxford, England, beckon the visitor to vistas of never-ending flights of fancy.

Overleaf: *Part of the spectacular parterre at Abbotswood, set with geometric skill by Sir Edwin Lutyens in the Cotswold landscape.*

Published by Clarkson N. Potter, Inc., and distributed by Crown Publishers, Inc., 201 East 50th Street, New York, New York 10022.

CLARKSON N. POTTER, POTTER, and colophon are trademarks of Clarkson N. Potter, Inc.

Manufactured in Japan.

Library of Congress Cataloging-in-Publication Data
Seebohm, Caroline.
    Private landscapes.

    Bibliography
    Includes index.
    1. Landscape gardening.   I. Sykes, Christopher Simon.   II. Title.
SB473.S46   1989   712   88-32432
ISBN 0-517-57261-3
10 9 8 7 6 5 4 3 2 1

First Edition

Acknowledgments

In early 1987 Carol Southern, Editor-in-Chief of Clarkson N. Potter, was having lunch with me after the publication of *English Country*. Over the salad, she allowed in her deceptively casual way as how she would like to do a garden book, one that would show the *whole* garden, not just bits of it. "Garden book?" I shrieked, tearing the napkin from my lap and leaping to my feet. "Gardening is the one subject I long to write about. Would you really . . . ?" Well she would, and it is her enthusiasm, encouragement, and curiosity that have taken us so exhilaratingly down the garden path.

Our gratitude goes first to the owners and gardeners, named and unnamed, who allowed us to enter their private landscapes and photograph them for this book. Their patience and understanding were exemplary; their gardens inspiring.

Special thanks go to Grace M. Hall, assistant to the late Thomas Church, who generously shared with us her knowledge of the master gardener, as well as her hospitality in California. We would also like to thank Mr. and Mrs. Robert Benton, Patrick Chassé, Mr. and Mrs. George R. Clark, Jim and Morley Clark, Anne and Joe Fox, Albert Francke, Andrew Leonard, Hitch Lyman, Lorne Michaels, Senga Mortimer, Patrick O'Connor, and Renée Vollen.

The troops at Clarkson N. Potter once again worked miracles, in particular, Ed Otto and Teresa Nicholas, designer Laurence Vétu-Kane, and Potter's Creative Director, Gael Towey, who was intriguingly weighed down with an as-yet unproduced volume of her own. Production editor Mark McCauslin caught the embarrassing textual gaffes that authors make when working too late at night after too many vermouths. Amy Schuler held the whole operation together with tact, efficiency, and good humor. Not many authors are so lucky in their life-support systems, and we thank them all.

You see, I believe that one ought always to regard a garden in terms of architecture as well as of colour. One has huge lumps of, let us say, the shrub roses making large voluminous bushes like a Victorian crinoline, or flinging themselves about in wild sprays; or, putting it another way, some plants make round fat bushes, and seem to demand a contrast in a tall sharp plant, say delphiniums, sticking up in a cathedral spire of bright blue amongst the roses instead of in the orthodox way at the back of a herbaceous border. It is all a question of shape.

Vita Sackville-West (1892–1962)

Contents

Gardens in the Landscape

Directory

PREFACE
by Caroline Seebohm

My impetus for writing this book came mainly from acquiring a house in New Jersey and wondering what on earth to do with the three acres of land surrounding it. The many garden books I consulted showed glorious photographs of gaudy borders, titillating topiary, romantic rose bowers, and watery walks, but failed utterly to give me any guidance in how to make sense out of my shapeless plot. This book, therefore, arises out of one novice gardener's need—an 18th-century need, if you like—to make order out of chaos.

There are some who oppose order in a garden, preferring an uncontrolled wilderness. Others feel that an open expanse of lawn stretching down to the road is all the garden one needs in this age of permanent rush-hour. There is talk now about the "new" American garden, which has no lawn or foundation planting, but instead drifts of perennials and ornamental grasses, unpruned hedges, low-maintenance shrubberies. This sounds to me rather like an "old" English garden. It also smacks suspiciously of fashion. Out with the marigolds and in with the sedums.

But making a satisfying garden is not directed by fashion. It is the expression of the owner's personal vision of the landscape, a vision inspired by his or her aesthetic sense of rhythm, color, and shape. You may yearn for a Dutch garden in California, or an Italian garden in Herefordshire. You may wish to look out of your surburban kitchen window at a Bolivian jungle. The gardens in this book, which come both from England and America, belong to their designers' individual dreams, carefully planted in the soil, and not to any passing fad. If there are rules, they are timeless and based on common sense.

My own garden remains shapeless, but I can see the future and it's going to be wonderful. For in spite of all the meticulous planning and planting, making a garden takes a long time, and you must be prepared to linger long enough to see it come to fruition. That's one of the strange things about gardeners. Along with their passion for compost, they assume longevity—and that's not such a bad way to live, after all.

PREFACE

by Christopher Simon Sykes

What powerful memories can be evoked by one's sense of smell. The scent of a rhododendron *fragrantissimum* the other day reminded me of my childhood, growing up in a house that always smelled of flowers. In the true tradition of the English country lady, my mother was a mad keen gardener, and she loved to have sweetly scented plants in the house all year round. She was able to do this because the octagonal walled garden in the grounds of our family home had large greenhouses, a number of which were heated to almost tropical temperatures, and a team of gardeners to fuss over their contents. The result was that spring came early to Sledmere House, with the first hyacinths coming in January, followed by daffodils and narcissi. Later on came the jasmine, the rhododendrons, and endless varieties of geranium, all filling the house with their heady aromas.

Although all of this gave me a great love of gardens, working on this book has been the hardest job I've ever undertaken. Gardens are notoriously difficult to photograph for a variety of reasons, not the least of them being that one is constantly at the mercy of the weather. This is particularly true in England, where one is likely to plan months in advance to visit a certain garden only to find black skies and teeming rain during the week in which it looks its best. A gray day dulls the colors, which tends to give the resulting photographs a lifeless look. Bright sunshine has much the same effect, giving them a flat appearance with little depth.

The composition of the picture can be difficult in that I cannot move shrubs and plants around to suit what I see through the view-finder, as I could objects or furniture when photographing an interior. Since the camera takes in only a fraction of what the eye does, the angle of approach is of vital importance, and in the one spot where I need to place the tripod there is inevitably a lake, a wall, or a large tree. But the real problem about taking photographs of gardens is that when one looks at the finished results, two vital elements are missing. No one can hear or smell a photograph, and what is a garden without the buzzing of bees and the heady scent of my rhododendron *fragrantissimum*? If there is any picture in this book that summons up these senses for the reader, only then do I judge it to be a success.

To build, to plant, whatever you intend,
To rear the Column, or the Arch to bend,
To swell the Terras, or to sink the Grot;
In all, let Nature never be forgot.
Alexander Pope (1688–1744)

INTRODUCTION

*In designing the layout, always approach it in a spirit of
adventure, enjoyment and also patience. Be bold and never be
put off by gloom-mongering friends who tell you that you will
never live to see the fruits of your creation. Even the making of
the garden will give untold pleasure.*

Sir Roy Strong (1935–   )

The healing powers of a garden have been extolled in art and literature since our earliest beginnings, when belief in the medicinal values of herbs and flowers prevailed, up to the present day, when sophisticated botanical and agronomic techniques allow us to experiment with almost any aspect of horticulture. Through the centuries, gardening styles have changed and evolved, but now there seems to be a new mood of urgency in the air, rooted in our growing sense of ecological crisis, the bleak prospect of industrial pollution and suburban blight, and our revived longing to escape from the worldly pressures of our daily lives. Gardens are being asked to do more than simply provide vegetables, culinary plants, or flowers for the table. We yearn for an earthly paradise, a "delicious retreat," as Voltaire put it, a direct line to Nature at a time when we feel dislocated from our universe.

There are now 25 to 30 million acres of cultivated lawn in America—a figure that gives some indication of the need for people to surround themselves with green grass. Scientist John H. Falk, an ecologist at the Smithsonian Institution investigating this phenomenon, found that there was a "deep innate preference for a grass landscape," even among those who had never been in a grassland setting in their lives. Among the most extensive grasslands in the world are the savannas of East Africa, where human beings first evolved. Dr. Falk concludes from this that we have a genetic predisposition for the surroundings of our earliest origins.

But the virtues of a garden do not lie in lawn alone. The creation of a garden springs from deep-seated needs of human beings, seeking solace from their worldly woes. Why else would the 17th-century writer Sir Richard Burton recommend walking in the garden as a respite from Melancholy? For the Persians, progenitors of the Western garden, the word *paradise* originally meant an enclosed hunting park and is still a Persian word for garden. Their elegant, watery oasis-gardens were an escape from the arid heat of the desert landscape. The Chinese saw their gardens as a symbolic expression of Man's attempt to be in harmony with Nature. The Italian Renaissance gardens were designed to provide intellectual stimulus as well as emotional satisfaction. For the French in the 18th century, the garden was not simply an arrangement of grass and greenery. It was a carefully laid-out system of appeasement and inspiration for Man's eternally troubled soul. As architect Philip Johnson has remarked, "All landscape architecture is hopeful architecture."

For those who scorn the philosophical argument, there are perfectly practical reasons for accepting the importance of what designers call "good bones" in a garden. Many experts say that well-designed landscaping can increase the value of residential property as much as 10 percent. New developments in rich sectors of the northeastern United States now routinely include estates of at least two to three acres plus parkland and ponds. A realtor in the property-booming center of New Jersey confirmed that what people are looking for today in new housing are exercise rooms, fireplaces, "and views, views, views." As an added incentive to house owners, a recent University of Utah study revealed that good landscaping presented a "psychological barrier" to potential burglars; hedges, walks, avenues of trees acting as a "symbolic lock" to the would-be intruder.

Views, hedges, walks, avenues—these are precisely the tools used by the great garden designers of history. To see what is meant by "bones," one only has to look at the plans of early Dutch, Italian, or English Renaissance gardens—elegantly aligned axes consisting of terraces, topiary, waterfalls, staircases, and arbors, all brilliantly connected by the symbolic mathematical grids of the Age of Reason, when God was in his Heaven, Man controlled Nature, and All was Right with the World. In those gardens, flowers and statues were secondary decoration added to complete the effect, just as fringe and tassels might be on drapery.

When Lancelot "Capability" Brown (1716–1783), a protégé of William Kent, and the supporters of the English landscape movement threw out all this formal structure (Brown hated all the fussy stonework and *parterres* up until then so fashionable), they threw out more than fringe and tassels. For Brown's ideas, largely developed from Kent's, required vast landscapes that could be artificially enhanced with lakes, clumps of trees, serpentine streams, and swaths of parkland. Brown's reckless journey from formality to the "natural" look changed forever the English countryside and influenced many Italian and French gardens as well.

A plan of a 17th-century Dutch garden, its ordered geometry typical of the period.

The 20th-century gardener, faced with shrinking space, expensive labor, and little time, could not compete with Brown's extravagances. While the Victorians helped bring back some of the lost formality, stylistic confusion reigned. One of this century's most distinguished landscape architects, the late Russell Page, referring somewhat tartly to Brown's "facile compositions of grass, tree clumps and rather shapeless ponds and lakes," was driven to the conclusion that "the formlessness of so many modern gardens stems from this earlier decadence." While the contemporary landscaping industry

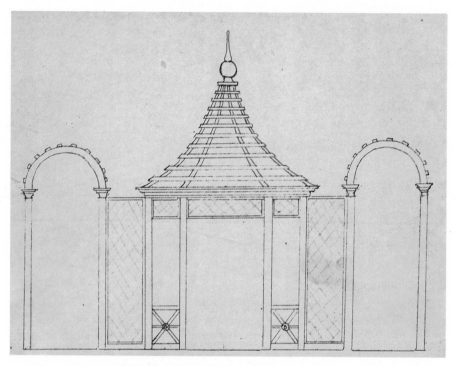

J. Liddon Pennock drawing for a pergola.

relies on clumps of yews ("spongelike excrescences," as Hugh Johnson describes them) pressed up against house walls, rows of evergreen shrubs in little mounds of wood chips, and carpets of blue rug juniper creeping across the ubiquitous lawn, the power of the garden remains in check, and our expectations of Nature frustrated. We long for relatedness, rhythm, equilibrium, and a sense of place in our encounters with the garden, and these elements are what the gardens in this book have been selected to express.

The smallest garden can look huge. The cheapest garden, expensive. The most low-maintenance garden as awesome as Versailles. The simplest garden can offer a healing and inspiriting experience. The gardens in the pages that follow prove these observations beyond a shadow of a doubt. They all delight the eye, provide rest, amusement, a feeling of space or enclosure, and most important of all, offer what the Chinese thought of as "refreshment for the heart." The layout might be a simple, geo-metric pattern, or an ambitious series of vistas, or a cottage-style border—but how well it is positioned and related to the given landscape is how well it will ultimately satisfy, and how long it will last. Even the ruined Renaissance gardens in Italy, with their crumbling staircases, overgrown *allées* of trees, and dry fountains, still retain some of their magic, thanks to the power of their original concept.

Perhaps it is not surprising, in view of the Italian influence, that the first use of the expression "landscape architecture" (as the title of a book by Gilbert Laing Meason in 1808) was in connection with Italian landscape painting. The phrase described the activity precisely, for the language of this kind of gardening is architectural—boundaries, verticals, texture, perspective, scale, containment, angles. Plants are chosen, not only for their color or hardiness, but also for their architectural qualities. Ilex, skyrocket juniper, buddleia, standard fruit trees, box, holly, cypress, yucca, euphorbia, linaria, mullein, gunnera, bergenia, are the living, growing pediments, columns, cornices, and gables, the "minarets and domes" as Vita Sackville-West described them, of the garden architect.

The most basic requirement for any project that involves architectural elements is, of course, a ground plan. Immediately the first-time gardener flinches. Garden plans are dry things, lines and squiggles on paper that bear no relation to the glorious effects one is hoping for. Yet it is a discipline that should be acquired, even if only at the most amateurish level. Most of the gardeners in this book sketched plans or had plans drawn up for them. What they tend to agree on, however, is that the plan alone will not make the garden. The plan should be examined on the site and reproduced with stakes, string, any technique that comes to hand for simulating the final result. (Painter Robert Dash, for instance, laid a sheet on the grass to see how a flower bed would look in that spot.) "As far as designing is concerned," says Rosemary Verey, author and designer of the gardens at Barnsley House in Gloucestershire, "I think it extremely difficult for anyone to be good at everything. When you see a design on paper, flat, maybe it looks wonderful, but you don't have the idea of elevations. The only way to discover that missing elevation is to walk in it."

Mrs. Verey has hit upon the other essential element in designing a garden, even a garden as formal and contrived as a knot garden. To walk "in" the elevation, so to speak, is to consult the *genius loci,* as Virgil described it, to pay homage to the mythical god or emperor who presides over your plot of land. The 18th-century poet and gardener Alexander Pope wrote a poem about the Genius of the Place, who:

Calls in the Country, catches op'ning glades,
Joins willing woods and varies shades from shades.

All the gardeners in this book refer in some way to the spirit of the place, directing their ideas, guiding their eye, suggesting shapes and rhythms in tune

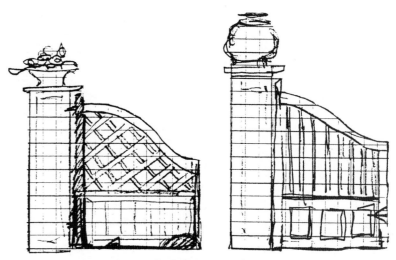

Nancy McCabe's ideas for gates.

with the landscape. As you walk in your garden, clutching your blueprints, the *genius loci* "paints as you plant, and, as you work, designs." Recognition of this mystical force seems to absolve us partly for our temerity in pitting ourselves against Nature. For as ecologists and environmentalists are only too aware these days, what we take from Nature is not without consequence. The exquisite sand mandalas created by Tantric Buddhists are ultimately swept up by them and poured back into the water whence the sand came—dust to dust. So must the gardener be prepared to accept that he is a tenant on this earth, and at some point dues must be paid.

The spirit of the place is friendly, not hostile, and generally has something helpful to say, particularly about the relationship between the garden and the house. This is where the garden plan plays its most important role. "The connection must be intimate," wrote Gertrude Jekyll, "and the access not only convenient but inviting." Indeed, ideally the house should be built at the same time as the gar-

These five sketches show how
Sir Roy Strong developed his
garden ideas.

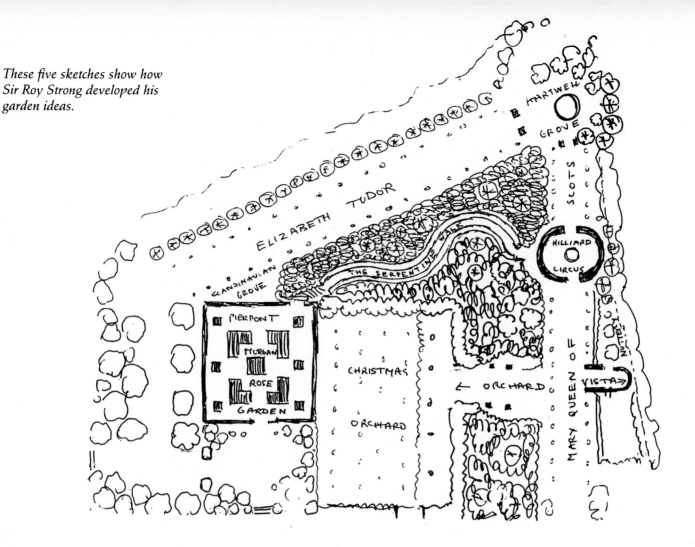

den, as was the case at the Villa Medici, Blenheim Palace, and Monticello, for instance, thus allowing complete harmony of siting, in terms of light, shade, proportion, and the surrounding landscape. "Notice how old houses and gardens are always beautifully related," says British designer David Hicks. "A good and successful garden, however new, will always have this sense of harmony." Oddly enough, many garden books show pictures of the gardens without any reference to the attendant house, thus disorienting the reader and undervaluing the design of the garden. In this book almost every story begins with the house, and how the house affected the development of the garden.

In a logical extension of this idea, many gardeners have regarded their gardens as outdoor rooms, simply extending the house into the landscape. The Chinese believed strongly in this concept, designing courtyards, pavilions, and galleries as a series of spaces for entertainment or contemplation. The famous English gardens at Sissinghurst and Hidcote are perhaps the foremost European examples of this notion. Sir Roy Strong carries this idea to the extent of saying that "planning a garden is similar to decorating and furnishing a house." A difference in this century, however, is that many people are accustomed to hiring an interior decorator to "do" their house, while even if an expert is consulted, the garden seems to plead for its owner's personal involvement.

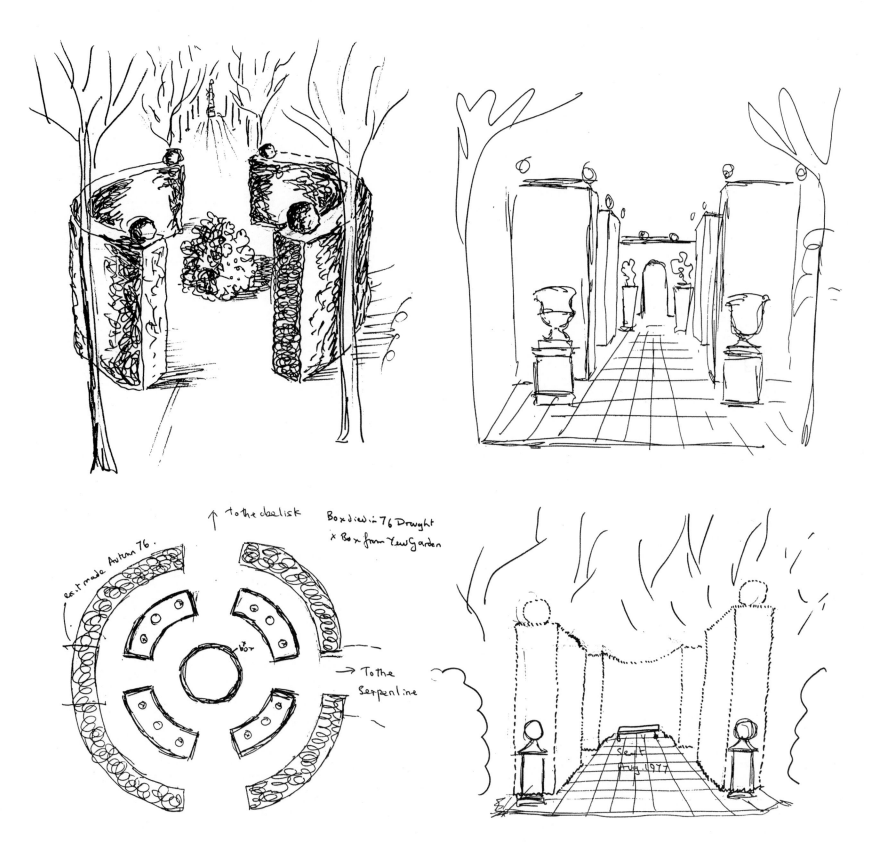

↑ to the obelisk

Box died in 76 Drought
x Box from Yew Garden

east made Autumn 76.

→ To the
Serpentine

Seat
Aug 1977

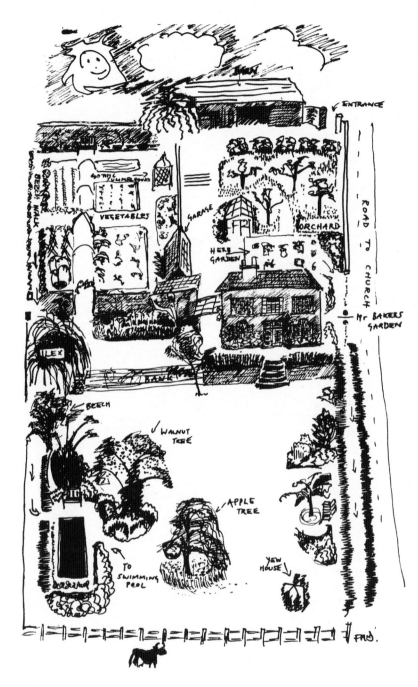

The labels in the illustration read:

ENTRANCE

ORCHARD

ROAD TO CHURCH

Mr BAKERS GARDEN

VEGETABLES

GARAGE

HERB GARDEN

ILEX

BEECH

WALNUT TREE

APPLE TREE

YEW HOUSE

TO SWIMMING POOL

FIN.

A charming rendering of Mary Keen's house and garden in Berkshire.

That is why gardening is such a delicious occupation. While many experts do it brilliantly, it is the amateur's dream. Sir Roy, like most of the gardeners represented in this book, is not a trained landscape architect. Academic qualifications are not required to pass tests with Mother Nature. While knowledge of botany, horticulture, and agriculture can enhance immeasurably a gardener's success rate, there are too many unknowns in gardening for it to be an exact science. It combines art with experimentation, nurture with nature, luck with skill, and provides an endless excuse to spend a lot of time wandering about one's backyard, thinking, sipping wine, imagining vistas, and communing with one's friend, the *genius loci.* All the gardener needs are a sense of mystery, of curiosity, of excitement, of romance, and of humor. To succeed also takes patience and a modicum of humility. If you do not have these qualities, your garden will remain earthbound.

If this sounds autocratic and opinionated, that is because most garden talk tends to be autocratic and opinionated. The gardeners who speak about their gardens in this book are autocratic, opinionated, and passionate. They have to be, to confront Nature, to endure the elements, to imagine the impossible, to sustain a vision, to accept losses, and to appreciate the occasional blessing. Gardeners tend to be like musicians—difficult, idiosyncratic, unworldly, but generous to a fault (it's almost impossible for one gardener to visit another without a plant or cutting being thrust into the visitor's hands upon departure), and deeply attuned to the clamor of the soul.

The voices in this book are startling in their disparity, and yet they share the same goal—to create a garden out of whole cloth, so to speak, to conjure out of the earth a living miracle. Even those inheriting famous or established gardens (Garsington and Sleightholmedale, for instance), who are denied the thrill of the *tabula rasa,* can still honor the past in the garden while adding new touches to make it their own. This is also true of the American corporate executive, who lives only a short time with his garden before being relocated, bequeathing the old and inheriting the new.

Whatever motivation brings us to embark upon a garden, "Green fingers are the extensions of a verdant heart," as Russell Page put it. For our gardens not only express us but also express the way we view the world. A Chinese garden evoked the world as a balancing act between God and Man. The Renaissance gardener was a Rationalist, at home in his universe. The English 18th-century stylist reinvented Nature in his art, and the Americans, from Thomas Jefferson to Frederick Law Olmsted, subtly manipulated the wild and waiting landscape to the country's benefit.

As for us, our place is less assured. Do we want enclosed spaces, fences, containment in our garden? Or do we want exuberance, overflowing borders, untamed woodland, vistas out to the horizon? Such choices reveal interesting inner lives and external assumptions about the world we live in. Over a garden doorway in Shanghai is written *T' an Yu'*—"To seek the mysterious." There could be no better invitation to enter the private landscapes included in this book, and afterward to return, refreshed and enlightened, to your own.

Out of all this the artist makes his own truth. Like his brothers back through history to the mythical Garden, he will re-create the landscape according to his own subjective image of reality. As he takes hold of earth, plants, and water, the materials unique to his art, let him only beware lest he destroy through his act of possession the genius of that which he has sought to possess.

Elizabeth B. Kassler, Modern Gardens and the Landscape, *1984*

Illustrator Nicola Bayley brings her talents to husband John Hilton's London garden.

SMALL-SPACE

No single element in the design of a garden is as important as where you put your paths. Once paths are made they dictate, not just to the feet but to the mind, the route to follow, the points from which the planting will be seen, indeed the whole shape of the garden.

Hugh Johnson (1939–)

GARDENS

A PAINTER'S TINY GARDEN OF

INFINITE VARIETY

MADOO

THE GARDENS OF ROBERT DASH

SAGAPONACK . NEW YORK

—— 1988 ——

P ainter Robert Dash believes that a garden is like a spiritual autobiography. "So making a garden," he declares, "means knowing who you are."

A tall order, perhaps, for us humble mortals, but Mr. Dash has much good advice as to how we may proceed in this task. "Give yourself a little questionnaire," he suggests. "For instance, when you go into a room, do you go left or do you go right? Are you a rapid person, or a lingerer? Do you like to sit or would you rather stand? Do you like things tall or short? Do you stroll, or do you run? Do you like things in your way, or a clear space

ahead of you? Do you like bright colors, or do you prefer no color at all? These are some questions to ask yourself when you figure out how to plan your garden."

Mr. Dash also believes that every piece of land speaks, and its special language must be discovered by its owner. "Start with no plans," he says. "Just walk around the land and think. Every garden has a resident emperor who makes the rules. Look at the shadows the house casts. Consider your neighbors. What are the nearest houses made of? Stone? Brick? Clapboard? What are the trees? Where are they? What is the landscape? Where is the nearest water?"

After communing with your plot comes the next step. "There are two age-old strategies for planning a garden," says the artist. "You can either go from the house OUT, or from the edge of the property IN. Either is all right. Start putting something down, make a mark. The size of your garden is unimportant. It's what you say within it that counts. A tiny space can be enormous. With good husbandry, you can make a small space infinite."

As to planting, there is one well-known gar-

Above: Beds planted with roses, phlox, iris, juniper, Mexican hollyhocks, globe thistle, and euphorbia are divided by brick paths contained, almost like a medieval garden, by the house and studio buildings.

Right: Wisteria foams down the side of the 18th-century barn/studio.

dener's test. Take a plant and put it in three places in your garden—the place you want it to grow, the place you think it should grow, and some other place you haven't even considered. "Needless to say," Robert Dash observes, "the place you haven't considered will be the place it grows beautifully!" And that, of course, must be its final location.

Mr. Dash has a further, more personal test, one that perhaps should be practiced with caution. "In making a garden we are dealing with microclimates," he explains. "Every garden has pockets of climate that differ from one another, and that will affect the life of your plants. Take your clothes off in midsummer and walk round your garden. Let the

A typical Dash vista, the arched path lined with a zigzag yew hedge, each angle planted with liriope, rue, sage, and santolina. The door, which came from an English castle, changes color on the whim of the gardener and his paintbrush.

air be still, and let it be night. You will at once feel the different temperatures on your skin. These are the microclimates to be observed by your plants.''

Naked or not, you will make mistakes. "You must make blunders. Everything that you plant can be ripped out—and that is perfectly all right. One idea is to take a lot of photographs of the garden and then take a pair of scissors and slice them up. Make a collage, move them around, see what happens. You must always experiment.''

Robert Dash's paintings use subtle splashes of color in large, fierce brush strokes. His latest work is almost all black, like deeply shadowed jungles interspersed with tiny specks of brilliant color, reflecting the philosophy of design in his garden. "There is no such thing as color in a garden,'' he says with typical fervor. "We are dealing with green on green on green, green shapes, green shadows, green geometry. Color is the last decoration, the last bedeckment. Think of the sculptural possibilities of a plant— solid, wavy, sticklike, tall, fat and so forth. This is the key to the shape you make of your garden.''

In his own Long Island garden he has designed a series of ''rooms'' around an old barn, dated 1740, that serves as Dash's studio and summer living quarters. From one side, the view looks out to a farm

with a flat expanse of field typical of eastern Long Island. Here he has designed a paved path with an obelisk at the end. "I had a line of yews at the end, but it was wrong. There's a natural geometry to the field, always being tilled, ploughed, planted. I wanted the view to stretch into that field."

As the gardens unfold, the mood changes from meadow to formality, from an Oriental water garden to a *potager,* or ornamental vegetable garden. Some plants are special favorites—the cardoon, Irish junipers, fastigiate ginkgo, *Rosa rubrifolia,* plume poppy, chicory, and monkshood. "Anything daisylike is my meat, but it must be mixed with the umbels of elephant garlic or second-year leek."

The manipulator is also the manipulated. "I do not like the look of a 'planned' garden, in spite of everything. Encourage a desire for a kind of deliberate awkwardness in your design—it works awfully well. To deliberately plant something off-center, against your instinct, expresses the same poetic idea as Emily Dickinson's 'Tell all the truth, but tell it slant.' I also have some dull areas in my garden, believing the eye must rest between excitements."

His planting is always natural looking, and he

The barn buildings act as a
frame for an inner courtyard
with views from each window.
Variety of color and shape is
achieved through the use of
broome, bamboo, shrub roses,
plume poppies, sidalcea, and
ornamental grasses.

A bright fence marks the parterre garden, designed with bricks and yew, with handsome Korean pots for decoration.

On the other side of the parterre garden, in complete contrast, an informal seating area. The designer likes to mix the formal with the informal. "It makes each more intense."

Opposite: *"I had always wanted a Moon Gate," says Mr. Dash, "but I said no, I'm not Japanese. Instead I latticed a tondo (a round painting) and set it behind a water tank, which is going to have yellow lotuses growing in it."*

Top: The mirrored woodshed is one of Robert Dash's more radical notions. "Why not? They reflect light, shade, the shape of the garden."

Right: A study in contrast— after man-made surprises, the gentle vista of a grassy meadowland walk.

Opposite: Two wooden bridges built by Mr. Dash, fringed with yellow irises and ferns, lead the way from the summer house and barn toward the winter house.

welcomes volunteers that pop up unexpectedly. "But remember, there is nothing natural about a garden. A garden is tamed nature. When I went to the Philadelphia Flower Show, I longed to open the doors and let all those little prisoners escape. When you make a garden, you confine nature. But nature has its rules too. That is what I mean by the resident emperor. You must accept those rules—the weather, for instance. Weather will always betray you, and you must work with it, not against it."

Robert Dash uses the paintbrush and the trowel with equal passion, for he sees that painting and gardening are the same. "They are gestural, they use the wrist, and they come from the heart." The artist makes his signature on the canvas and also in the soil. In his 1.91 fascinating acres, his spiritual autobiography is in plain view for all to see.

From the winter house, the dining room window looks out onto a forced-perspective path (eight feet wide at the near end, narrowing to six feet) anchored by an obelisk.

Left: A Robert Dash painting of the landscape shows his passion for shape, form, and subtle hues.

Right: This gently curving grass patch makes an interesting contrast with the geometric vista above.

The lastest addition, the pergola, is covered in laburnum, and a fountain will be placed in the center. To the right the hedge has fenestrations—little gaps to let the light in and open up space.

A METICULOUSLY PLANNED
ILLUSION OF GRANDEUR

Meadowbrook Farm was built in 1936. Its owner, J. Liddon Pennock, Jr., was then 22 years old. He and his wife, Alice, have lived here and been working on the garden ever since. The results of that 50-year gestation can be seen in every corner of Mr. Pennock's masterpiece of design. Not that this longevity should daunt the more mobile or part-time gardener. What makes Mr. Pennock's garden so astonishing is not only its size—it is less than two acres—but that he makes changes every year, every month, almost every day, thus proving that with a strong structure, the look of permanence and mellowness can be achieved practically overnight.

The garden is a series of small "rooms," which flow into one another, cut out of a very steep hillside, surrounded by woods, and connected by axes —lines and angles creating vistas and visual interest for the visitor. The whole tiny landscape is ornamented with elaborate waterworks, gates, steps, statuary, and gazebos. This description is an almost exact blueprint for an Italian Renaissance garden, in which the combination of statues, fountains, wooded vistas, and grottoes, all laid out in perfect proportion, provided a symbolic representation of Man's position at the center of the Universe.

"You can only see each part of the garden where you are supposed to see it," declares Mr. Pennock, reflecting the Renaissance view of Man's control over his environment. The design originates from the house itself and is mathematically aligned with each facade. Thus out of each window of each room, a different view has been created. All the walks and walls either line up with the house or are at right angles to it. And radiating out from each axis, a different vista forms, often crowned by the

The Eagle Garden, named for the marble eagle that raises its wings over an oval lawn, with geometrically carved beds at the four corners. Beyond is a steep drop down into the wooded hillside below.

Right: The eagle is guarded by unusually pruned yews, trained to turn inward, creating a dramatic bonsai effect.

Far right: The tender dracaena in this urn is in a removable pot, thus easily wintered over.

careful placement of a statue or a gazebo. There are seven gazebos in the garden, many of which Mr. Pennock designed and built himself, adding a specific feeling of period to the atmosphere.

In spite of this crowded inventory, standing in one part of the garden the visitor cannot guess what is to come. This is again the influence of Renaissance gardening—to introduce the element of surprise. The planning involved here is remarkable. "I used to walk around all the time with a tape measure," explains the designer. "Setting up the correct angles takes accurate measuring. I also had to create a flow between each part of the garden. There is the right way to enter and to leave each of our little 'rooms.' You never have to retrace your steps."

The effect of this subtle manipulation is to give the visitor the sense that the garden is much bigger than it in fact is—the goal of most backyard gardeners and the triumph of good landscape design. The maintenance, Mr. Pennock insists, is minimal. This is hard for the visitor to believe. But there are no herbaceous borders, no large stretches of lawn, only a lot of ivy, ground cover, and container-grown plants that winter indoors. (The urns, for instance, are filled with removable pots, rather than soil-filled plantings.) "I have basically no flowers. Just lots of bedding plants, a few perennials. The only maintenance this garden requires is pruning." In proof, he never leaves the house without his pruning shears. "Every shrub or bush that goes in must be planted so it doesn't hide things. We lop off lower limbs, thin out the top, ruthlessly take away branches to create the right shape. Or as the English say, 'prune up, take down.'"

The most difficult design aspect of the Meadowbrook garden is invisible—the engineering feats required in cutting the level garden areas out of the extremely steep hillside. "The slopes were very hard to work with," concedes Mr. Pennock, "but the dramatic terracing is far more satisfying than flat terrain.

Top: A small terrace to the left of the Eagle Garden offers a shady retreat, reflecting, as everything in this garden does, some aspect of the house.

Above: Near the terrace is a small dipping pool, heated and installed with a Jacuzzi. Lush evergreen planting and topiary provide privacy.

A detail of the sedum planter in the center of the Herb Garden, surrounded by four different kinds of lettuce, plus sage, rosemary, ligularia, figs, and other herbs.

Opposite: The Herb Garden, designed and laid out in the Elizabethan manner by the owner. Hemlock and santolina act as hedges. Brick paths and Brazilian red shale form the walkways.

Top left: *Mr. Pennock's unusual treatment of this row of* Poncirus (Citrus trifoliata) *in the Lower Garden turns them into spectacular lollipops.*

Top right: *The evergreen conifer* Cedrus atlantica glauca, *planted on the other side of the wall, has been trained to flow dramatically down the* allée *side of the wall like a waterfall.*

Above left: *The vista on the Upper Terrace is completed by a mock-Oriental gazebo.*

Above center: *The gazebo, which Mr. Pennock enhanced with black and gold paint, looks out over a black-painted armillary. (He often paints his urns and statuary black for artistic effect.)*

Above right: *Perched above the steep wooded hillside in the Lower Garden, this reproduction neoclassical stone and wrought-iron gazebo makes an elegant finale to yet another visual journey in the Pennock garden.*

Every time we dug out one side of the hill we filled up the other side. We were forced to install a retaining wall to support the level ground."

Liddon Pennock had no formal training as a landscape gardener, but comes rather from the tradition of gifted amateurism that was the foundation of English gardening and that often produces the finest results. He studied agronomy and horticulture at Cornell University, but his real training came from working with his father, who ran a florist's shop in Philadelphia. Growing up among all those flowers turned the son into a gardener, one whose extraordinary sense of design comes from instinct, com-

An enchanting scene where plants and statuary combine to produce another dazzling effect.

bined with a solid sense of mathematics.

One might suppose that having produced such a wonderful garden over almost half a century, Mr. Pennock might sit down and enjoy it. A true gardener, however, never rests. "I did this garden bit by bit. We go on adding and adding. We have a new fountain this year, for instance. The vista from the swimming pool toward the driveway is another new creation." He wonders whether to paint an urn black, add a lilac walk, pull out a dwarf blue spruce planting. His eye is always searching for another excitement, an improved vista, a change in perspective. An extra task which he likes to do, although not required for maintenance, is to change the bedding plant schemes from month to month as the seasons change. For this, plus the minimal mowing, he enlists the help of a two-day-a-week gardener.

Apart from the garden, Mr. Pennock runs a large commercial nursery, which provides plants for wholesalers and designers all over the United States. "I just wanted to be able to supply my own cuttings and seedlings," he says, gazing in some astonishment at the rows of greenhouses and workers scurrying about carrying plants and merchandise orders. His wisdom and generosity have given the whole country a gift, which is expressed most vividly in his own small but brilliant garden.

Opposite and above: The planting in the Round Garden changes with the seasons. The fountain in the center achieved its ancient look with the help of cow manure, cider vinegar, and lampblack.

Below: A grassy walk to the right of the pool pavilion leads to this Pennock-designed gazebo, marbleized in greens and yellows to match the plants that grow nearby.

FROM A BACKYARD OF RUBBLE

TO A GREEN AND LEAFY JUNGLE

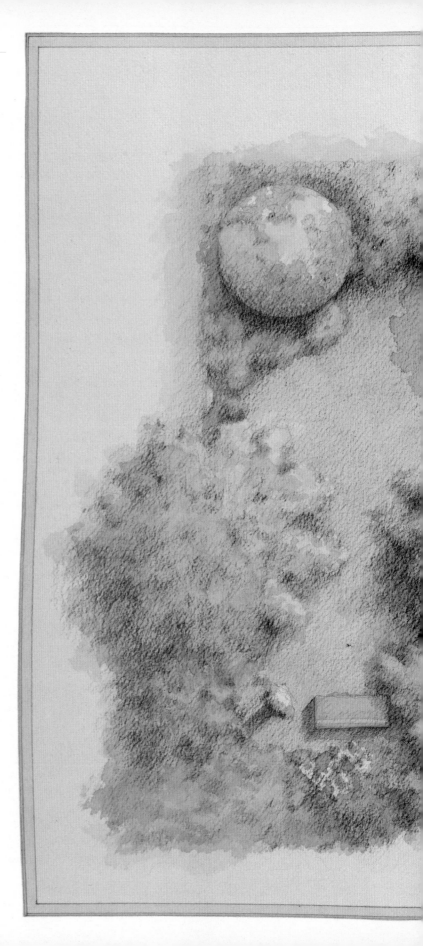

The site was unpromising—a scrubby wasteland, reminiscent of an urban dump, not much sun, no soil to speak of, and an uninspiring 80-by-40-foot rectangular shape to play with. A nightmare for a house person perhaps, but a gift for the imaginative gardener, a gift that John Hilton, a young barrister, snapped up in 1972 as though he were being offered a piece of the Berkshire Downs.

"I always longed to make a garden," he says. "I saw it all—an all-year-round garden with raised beds, shrubs, climbers, white flowers, and the accent on overall shapes." Such a picture must have threatened to fade at times when the earth moving began. The whole yard had to be leveled, then the beds

Opposite: The rear of this London house looks out onto a dappled green landscape remote from the city's noise and hubbub. On the left is the kitchen, on the right the living room, with entrances into the garden from both areas.

Left: Seen through a window, the garden is formed out of dense shrubbery, sculpture, and an ornamental pond close to the house, opening up to a lawn stretching away toward the far end of the property.

made with secondhand granite blocks (cobblestones from London streets purchased from the city authorities), and layers of topsoil added (plus peat mixed with leaf mold taken from local woods). But John Hilton had a strong sense of what he wanted to do with the 80-by-40-foot rectangle, and his vision never wavered.

"I made a long bed along the length of one side, and coming out from the other side I built a peninsular bed that jutted out across the center of the garden."

This simple piece of carving-up miraculously changed everything. It instantly provided two gardens instead of one, gave the illusion that the space was much larger than it was, offered a pleasing vista from the house, and added a totally concealed area on the other side of the peninsula to intrigue the visitor. From the original rectangle, then, John Hilton created a series of shapes, lines, and views that

The lily pond is stocked with goldfish, watched over by a nameless marble gentleman, shaded by a pale Acer japonicum aureum, *and* surrounded by shade-loving plants such as ferns, euphorbia, and hosta.

turned his thankless backyard into a gardening adventure. Such is the power of the landscaper's art.

The next step was to make a pond outside the back of the house. The soil dug out from the hole was mounded up around the sides, thus giving height to beds around the water, which was soon well stocked with fish, frogs, and toads. The brick walls surrounding the garden were given a decoration of climbing plants. The only extravagance Mr. Hilton allowed himself was to buy and plant two mature 25-foot trees, a western hemlock and a triple-trunked silver birch, to conceal the high brick wall of a warehouse at the far end, that could be seen from the house. All the other trees and shrubs went in small. But a good garden designer knows per-

Above left: The cast-iron steps leading up to the kitchen were retrieved from an old Victorian house. Variegated ivy and a chimney pot containing honeysuckle create a green arch.

Top: John Hilton calls this the Bower, with its stone seat surrounded by ivy and jasmine officinale *and* polyanthum.

Above: The view from the kitchen looking along the back of the house, punctuated with yucca and a grouping of terra-cotta containers at the far end of the path.

A shady arch protects the kitchen steps into the garden.

Above right: *The temple is flanked by yucca in urns, palms, a climbing loquat (grown from a pit saved by Mr. Hilton after eating the fruit in Spain),* Trachycarpus fortuneii *smuggled out of Japan in a sponge bag, and at the extreme left, a group of silver birches.*

Opposite: *This stone-carved Venetian Turk was found at a Rutland country house sale. Mr. Hilton removed bricks in the wall and cemented the Turk in place, then painted the bricks to make them look old.*

fectly well how they will grow and look in only a few years' time. "All it takes is patience," says John Hilton.

One further conceit was introduced—a temple and colonnade to create the focal point of the extended vista toward the bottom of the garden. John Hilton, scavenger par excellence, gathered his columns from salvage operations and old building sites and installed them along the far wall. His temple was also built column by column—the pièce de résistance being the dome, somewhat more elusive to acquire. "The compromise was presented by a fiberglass-lampshade maker in Paddington: there is not much difference between making a large lampshade and one measuring eight feet in diameter."

Thus were the bones laid for what might have been simply an urban backyard. The dressing, or clothing, was just as carefully planned and followed through. John Hilton wanted a green and gray gar-

Left: *These snapshots of the house and garden show with what brilliant feat of imagination John Hilton took the place and transformed it, and how he carefully mapped and carved, dug and planted, until he achieved his masterly results.*

Right: *Sculpture gives a focal point to shaded areas of the garden.*

Below left: *A Victorian young woman gazes over a green landscape of ivies and camellias.*

Below right: *A marble Doge contemplates his surroundings, which include hebe, ferns, camellias, and jasmine.*

Opposite: *At the far end of the garden, beyond the peninsula bed and past the temple, the visitor may finally rest in this colonnaded corner, which is planted with* Cornus alba, Laburnum, *and* Viburnum plicatum tomentosum.

den, and all his shrubs, plants, trees, and flowers had to adhere to his strict plan. Shape—texture—color —scent—these four elements dominated his choices for plants, and the results are as dramatic and varied as any Nature has to offer. Ferns, ivies, acers, yucca, jasmines, lilac, camellias, rue, euphorbia—nothing exotic or out-of-the-way here, familiar plants with familiar names. But planted in abundance and with an eye always rigorously on the lookout for shape, size, and texture, they take on a kind of grandeur. "A lesson I learned was to think and make big," says John Hilton. "It is important not to create puny beds and apologies for planting areas." No apologies, indeed, are required for this brilliantly conceived and executed small garden.

A FORMAL GARDEN IN A HOT, DRY CLIMATE

This garden in northern California, designed by Thomas D. Church, uses a series of axes and angles reminiscent of the great Italian Renaissance gardens. The house in fact was designed around an Italian cypress tree planted in what was to become a glass-walled inner atrium of the house. (The tree later grew so large that it had to be removed.) This set the theme for the architecture of the garden, which is really a series of spaces, or rooms, each one leading the visitor farther into the garden. The first "room" is the atrium, surrounded by a gallery of fine paintings collected by the owners. The atrium also contains a quatrefoil pool and fountain, and orange trees, typically Mediterranean.

From this serene garden-atrium the visitor steps through glass doors onto a terrace, also decorated with orange trees. The paving for the terrace was laid in diagonal squares, to contrast with the rectangular shape of the pool area beyond. "Our terraces today must be in scale with what we expect them to do for us," Thomas Church declared. This one is quite small, providing no threat to the proportions of the pool, which is the focal point of this garden.

Positioning pools remains tricky in most garden designs, since the pool is basically an intractable object that has to be installed and serviced in a scientific fashion. Thomas Church put a great deal of thought into his pools, integrating them into the surroundings as carefully as possible. "Being the largest

The patio of this California house acts as a transition between the inner atrium (seen through the glass doors on the left) and the pool. A comfortable outdoor room, it is dominated by a potted orange tree.

Right: From the patio, one looks out onto the serene contours of Thomas Church's pool and, beyond it, a background of tall green trees.

single design element in the composition, the pool cannot be hidden or disregarded on properties of an acre or less. Its success or failure, aesthetically, will depend on where it is placed, what forms are chosen as being most sympathetic to the site, what materials will do the most to heighten possible dramatic effects and blend most harmoniously with the house and the distant landscape.''

Mr. Church raised this pool above the level of the terrace, thus giving it the stature of an ornamental pool. He added a fountain at the end and surrounded it with choice sculpture, echoing the great gardens of 16th-century Italy. Thomas Church al-

The inner atrium of the house has a quatrefoil pool and fountain in the Italian style, and all four walls are made of glass, creating a light-filled gallery for the owners' fine collection of contemporary art.

The pool, with its flights of steps and dark interior, has the quality of a reflecting pool as seen in Mughal gardens. The focal point at the far end, a statue by Barbara Hepworth, is accentuated by another staircase, and the dark background of shrubs highlights the elegant form of the sculpture.

Below: *A contemplative bronze by Greek sculptor George Pappas is an elegant adornment to the pool.*

Opposite: *The blowsy blooms of the rose garden add color and informality to the left-hand side of the garden, in contrast to the serene center with its shimmering pool.*

ways liked sculpture in a garden and believed that it was not used enough. People today seem still to be afraid of it, although, as he said, "After greenery, nothing, I believe, enhances a garden more than sculpture."

He also liked steps, which "produce emotion," and as in this case, add drama and interest, inviting the visitor to leave the terrace and walk up to the welcoming coolness at poolside. The dark color of the interior water blends well with the landscape, and at the far end of the pool, mature trees give the feeling of protection and shade.

There are, however, those who will look at this central garden landscape and wonder at the amount of stone slabs or cement that greet the eye. Compared to gardens on the East Coast of the United States, for instance, or even more strikingly, to the gardens of England, Mr. Church's layout seems austere, cold, lacking in effusiveness. Yet the challenge of making plants grow without regular rainfall is forgotten by those who do not garden under such conditions. (Even if an elaborate irrigation system has been installed, the water supply may not be capable of fueling it.) Sometimes Californians themselves will forget and start making a flowery, grassy

garden, only to see it decimated by drought. Even if annuals are watered, the flowers may die early and leave holes in the beds. Such experiences are discouraging and often deter the novice plantsman.

Thomas Church knew better than most the impossibility of making an English garden in a desert climate. Instead he used paving rather than lawn, textures rather than borders, fire-retardant plants and succulents rather than thirsty perennials. (Such selections also reduced maintenance by a considerable margin.) Yet he usually managed to find lush, verdant spots in his landscapes. In this layout, while the pool provides the calm, central focus of the garden, on each side lie other, contrasting delights, woody and wild. To the left of the pool is a rose garden and wisteria-covered arbor, giving color to the otherwise neutral palette of the garden. To the right is a winding walk, leading up a gentle hill through shrubs to another sculpture and a charming vista back to the pool. Two modest strips of lawn provide a green carpet on each side of the pool.

Off the study, at the side of the house, is yet another garden "room," this time a small oasis of shade in the Oriental style. This secret garden's concept comes from the Chinese idea that the more intimate you become with the garden's owner, the more you may be permitted to penetrate into the most private corners of his garden—and, by extrapolation, his soul.

Rhythm and movement are essential. You expect them in the pictures you hang on your wall, in the music you listen to, in the poetry you read. In the garden it's the wind in the foliage and the dog running across the lawn. It's the line of the terrace and the repetition of richly textured foliage. The eye is a restless organ.

Thomas D. Church (1902–78)

Top: *A woodland path traverses the whole perimeter of the garden, planted with spring bulbs, native irises, lilies of the valley, weigelas, and forget-me-nots.*

Above: *The path winds up a gentle slope around toward the right-hand side of the garden, high shrubs concealing the view.*

The end of the woodland walk brings the visitor to a small statue with spring plantings. A hedge acts as a screen for this little bower.

Right: Thomas Church used many textures in this garden—concrete around the pool, gravel, rocks, and neat edgings for paths and beds to allow for easy maintenance. Surrounding this woodland garden is a high wire fence to protect it from intruders—invisible since it is painted black, Church's preferred color for making fences disappear.

AUSTERE ANGLES WITH
VOLUPTUOUS PLANTING

This is a professional garden designer's own garden, and it shows. No wasted space, no excessive color, no jarring lines, no mismatched styles. Nancy McCabe started, as all good designers do, with the house, a small Connecticut farmhouse she and her husband bought five years ago. Its simple, unglamorous, stucco and wood-trim facade rises above a steep hillside. The house fed Mrs. McCabe's passions—straight lines, an overview, climbing plants such as wisteria and clematis, massed borders, country-garden flowers in pastel shades—and she saw how in this unpromising plot she could include them all. Hers is a textbook story of the making of a small but wonderful garden.

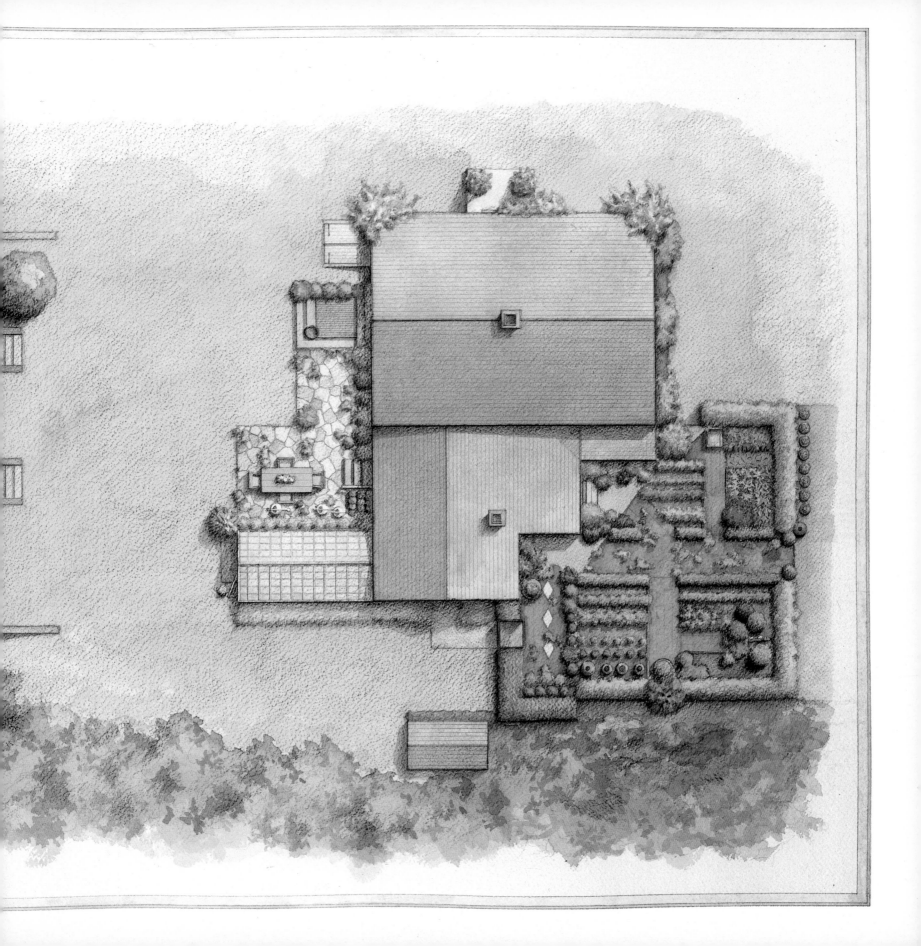

"It's very important that a garden and a landscape evolve," she says. "Nothing can be done overnight. If we start with the area around the house first, then move slowly outward, the land will tell us what to do. That is why every garden is so different.

"When I first came to this house there was literally nothing. No one had lived in it for years and years. It was neglected and unloved. There was no garden. There were no walls. The grass was three feet high. But I loved it at once. I knew I wanted a garden I could look down on. Some of my favorite gardens, like the Paca House in Annapolis, which I have always adored, have been designed like this. You can be almost anywhere and look down on a lower level. This house offered me my overview."

The major landscaping plan was to terrace the land on the south side of the house to make a lawn, and then to cut a rectangular garden out of the sharply sloping and crumbling hillside. This at once provided a terrace outside and grass near the kitchen and living-room doors, with the eye being led down toward the surprising drop into the fenced garden beneath.

The wall that encloses the lower garden is made of stucco and framed in wood, to reflect the architecture of the house, with two stairways into the garden, also made of wood with lattice risers to match those on the steps to the kitchen and living-room doors. "The wooden fence that butts against the stucco wall on its two outside ends is tall enough to give a feeling of enclosure without any grandness. That was important as our house has nothing grand about it." Meticulously following the design lines given by the house, she also chose an extremely plain fence, with no finials.

The contrast between this unfussy bone structure and the massed borders it contains is heightened by the depth of the beds—a little over four feet, significantly large, thus allowing flowers to bush and spill over in luxuriant abandon. All Mrs.

Opposite: *This basic farmhouse has been wonderfully enriched by the addition of gardens both in front and in back, enveloping it in a green and growing landscape. The kitchen garden, seen here, is a triumph of geometry, restraint, and abundance.*

Above: *A simple pot of lavender can look like a fragrant jungle.*

Right: *A trellis arch acts as link between the kitchen garden on the northeast side of the house and the main landscaped garden on the south side. The arch also affords a pleasing framed vista of each garden.*

Below: *A variety of pots hold herbs, with four standard bay trees standing guard behind them.*

The greenhouse, given designer status with its neat rows of watering cans and young dianthus in training wires, is winter repository for many of Nancy McCabe's tender plants, such as rosemary, agapanthus, moonflowers, and the splendid Passiflora caerulea *seen here on the extreme left, outside enjoying the summer climate.*

Far left: *Inside, the greenhouse waits for its winter treasures.*

Left: *An old garden chair wears its age with dignity.*

McCabe's favorite flowers make an appearance here; single hollyhocks, bleeding hearts, ornamental catnip, apricot foxgloves, *Salvia argentea,* violas, mixed with herbs such as tarragon, garlic chives, and fennel. She also loves fragrant lilies, heliotrope, pinks, nicotiana, and sweet rocket. Yet there is a remarkable harmony of color. She talks as designers talk about a color palette, and about a plant's architecture (Scotch thistles and Siberian iris, for instance, giving strength to the softness of other foliage). The results seem natural, yet always interesting.

Turning back to look up at the house, one's eye is led to a charming greenhouse attached to the house, built by Nancy McCabe's husband of materials from an old cypress greenhouse. Mrs. McCabe specializes in standards, and in this greenhouse she grows and trains them, along with other plants and cuttings that must be wintered over. Thus the garden is full of surprises—*Convolvulus mauretanicus, Passiflora caerulea,* standard rosemary, agapanthus, moonflowers—hardly what one would expect to see blooming in northwestern Connecticut.

The kitchen garden was worked on last, but probably most lovingly of all. Nancy McCabe had a collection of old garden tiles found in Savannah and she edged her paths with these. Her inspiration for the layout came mostly from France, where she at-

Above: *A pretty grouping of pots includes lavender, carnations, pansies, and Passiflora caerulea.*

Above right: *Detail of watering can and mullein, with dianthus in training.*

Opposite: *Meticulously laid-out beds in the herb garden, with pots of winter-tender plants and a red currant hedge.*

tended school. "I saw no beautiful flowers in France, but many grand plans, and those are just as influential to a garden designer." She remembers in particular the sensational vegetable gardens at Villandry and Versailles. Yet her most vivid memory of all was a simple kitchen garden on the road to the famous French chateau. "It was beyond all I could imagine! There were rows and rows of young tender plants covered with cloches. There must have been at least seventy-five in all. Some had broken knobs and small clay pots perched on top to anchor them, which only added to their charm. I don't think I've seen any garden that touched me more."

The vegetable garden area is tiny (perhaps 25 feet square), but as neat and ordered as you would expect from such a visual perfectionist. In defiance of her own preference for overplanting in her big perennial borders, in the kitchen garden nothing spills over. Soil is quite clearly seen in between the

Opposite: *A sculpted lead planter embraces a riot of imperial pink pansies.*

Below: *An unusual collection of planters, lidded and otherwise, mostly used for wintering over tender specimens.*

lettuces and the rows are as geometric as a T square. Counteracting this formality is a planting of flowers alongside the vegetables—a combination also seen in the perennial borders.

The garden is now five years old. "Each year I change things slightly. Friends give me seeds, such as *Verbena bonariensis* and *Saliva patens.* I keep cutting things back that seem to take over, like *Rosa gallica.* I took a couple of box bushes from another garden I had in New York State, and I have to keep accommodating them as they get larger. I change my garden if people I love give me plants. I keep adding. For instance, the shrubbery beyond the perennial gardens is mainly pink and white, but now I've added blue-flowering caryopteris, white buddleia, and white Rose of Sharon ("Diana") to extend the season of bloom. And to maintain privacy, I've put in more white pines to screen us from next door." (Ironically, since this planting, the McCabes have bought the house next door and painted it gray with white trim and dark teal doors. It will be used for Nancy's office.)

While working on her own garden, Nancy McCabe is also working hard for her many clients. "One of the reasons I enjoy working on other people's gardens is because I can do all the things I can't do in my own. People must think I'm this madwoman who adores brick courtyards and walls. I can't do them here and so I love to do them for other people!"

She thinks gardeners today are far more knowledgeable than a generation ago, many having visited the great gardens in England and Italy for inspiration. Her only piece of advice is the familiar but difficult one—be ruthless. "One of the things I loved about Vita Sackville-West was her saying that if you don't like it, rip it out. Gardeners tend to move plants rather than get rid of them. But if you have lots of cotoneaster or creeping juniper, I wouldn't hesitate—rip them out!"

Opposite, clockwise from top left: The lower garden, on the south side of the house, entered by two stairways from the terrace; pots of Convolvulus cneorum *mark the steps; below, massed borders of flowers and herbs. From the terrace, the sunken garden can be seen, framed by a simple fence, with woodland beyond. From the wooded area, one looks back toward the house, the plain stucco architecture reflected in the wall delineating the perimeter of the garden. A corner of the sunken garden, showing a profusion of plants including hollyhocks, sweet rocket, lilies,* Salvia argentea, *lavender, and, in the spring, irises, tulips, and coral bells.*

Top left: A long view of the formal garden, showing the perspective of terrace, lawn, garden, and woods.

Left: On the other side of the formal sunken garden, a wooden seat encircles a tree.

Containers

Growing plants in pots is an age-old gardening custom. When the original gardens were planned for Longleat House in Wiltshire in the late 17th century, 2,500 potted plants were arranged in the *parterre* in front of the house. The visitor to the Humble Administrator's Garden in Soochow, China, gasps in admiration at the massed banks of chrysanthemums, only to discover that every single one of them is planted in a pot. The Chinese have always loved moveable color and flexible forms, as we do today.

Container plants not only resolve problems of barren soil or inconvenient spaces, but also allow the gardener to grow non-hardy blooms that when summer is over may be brought indoors in their pots until after the last spring frost. As well as these advantages, potted plants offer the garden, like a vase of flowers in a room, an infinite variety of changing shapes and colors through-out the seasons.

Unusual Use of Plants

A gardener learns that plants, like dogs, can be trained to do almost anything, with a certain amount of care and patience. Standard roses, lime trees on stilts, hollies like lollipops, ivy trellises, topiaries—these are just a few of the unusual growth patterns experts impose on plants for the purpose of enhancing the garden.

Along with such structural changes, plants may also be persuaded to grow under strange conditions invented by their ingenious owners. A potted plant may hang from a branch; a shrub emerge from a paving stone; a tree explode with purple flowers. Victorian bedding techniques evolved from this unconventional attitude toward plants and planting. Why not pack 50 sweet williams in the ground together to make a scented mattress? Why not write your name in lobelia? This is, of course, the opposite of the currently fashionable mode of "natural" gardening. The choice remains. Plants are surprisingly adaptable. Only one thing is certain—a topiary bird will never fly away.

Clockwise from top right: *Chionanthus as a standard. Fuchsia rises like a tree from its buried pot. Cedrus atlantica glauca trained down a wall like a waterfall. Poncirus pruned like lollipops. Wisteria meets iris in a purple pattern. Variegated dogwood meets variegated weigela contrary to conventional rules.*

GREEN AND WHITE ROOMS IN A SMALL CITY GARDEN

A late-Georgian row house in London faced on one side the street, and on the other a wide, rectangular backyard garden. The architectural layout of the back of the house is L-shaped—the L being a small addition to the house on the right that could be rented as a separate apartment. Otherwise the design was typical of the period—redbrick terrace outside the back door, and a flat lawn stretching the length of the property, with inevitable views of adjacent house walls each side and at the far end. The garden's planting consisted mostly of a seven-foot-high line of Queen Elizabeth roses, and a valuable cherry tree.

The present owner disliked most of what she

Top: *Another angle of the garden, showing the second room with its central box-framed roundel.*

Above: *The reverse view, seen from a window inside the house before the gazebo was installed.*

Opposite: *View of the back of the house from the gazebo at the far end of the garden, showing the major axis of the design and the high evergreen hedges dividing the two "rooms."*

saw, in particular her neighbors' walls, the roses (her least favorite hybrid), and the boring expanse of lawn. "We called it the golf course," she remembers. The solution was to alter drastically the shape of the terrain. "I wanted to make a series of rooms," she says. "It has always been my favorite form for a garden."

Landscape architect Arabella Lennox-Boyd (author of *Traditional English Gardens*) and her then-partner Michael Balston (author of *The Well-Furnished Garden)* worked in stages to carve out proper bones in this unimaginative landscape. "The garden was divided according to the architecture of the house, which really offered one central flank and two side flanks," says Mrs. Lennox-Boyd. "Because of the width of the garden, we were able to divide it into three—a shade garden outside the drawing room on the left, a central garden that ran along the main axis of the house, and a simple, third garden that belonged to the separate apartment on the right."

The designers planted high hedges along the left side, which succeeded in concealing the next-door walls. Along this side the shade garden offers seclusion from the rest of the world. A new, pleached lime-tree screen diminishes the neighbors' walls on the opposite side, where a grass path was formed to run the length of the garden.

The four borders, which defined the first new section or "room" of the garden, were then dug and planted, and four crab apple trees were placed inside this new room, as architectural focal points, with an underplanting of Japanese anemones. The designers kept strictly to the classical forms, working out axially from the back door of the house to the end of the garden. The first "room" ends halfway down the garden, the division marked by two evergreen hedges like a low wall, with a narrow opening through which one glimpses the far end of the garden. A path bisects the garden horizontally between the two hedges.

On the other side of these hedges, a second "room" was added later with four more beds sculpted out of the lawn. This second space was given form by a central roundel, outlined in box, with a small evergreen obelisk planted at its heart. A new white rose garden has recently been planted in one of the beds.

Meanwhile the brick terrace was replaced with a larger flagstone patio, surrounded with shade-loving plants such as hydrangeas, hellebores, hostas, bergenias, and outlined with a trellis decorated with

Opposite: A fierce guardian rests at the foot of the terrace steps, in front of a tangle of greenery.

Left: One of the four box-framed beds in the first section of the garden, in which are planted a crabapple tree and a ground-cover ruff of Japanese anemones.

Below: A pleached lime screen helps to conceal the neighbors, while climbing roses tumble over a rustic seat.

Overleaf: The formal second room, alight with white crambe and roses, yellow phlomis, the still-new pergola draped with wisteria.

Albéric Barbier climbing roses. This trellis also serves as a doorway into the sequence of outdoor rooms beyond.

The planting choices for the entire garden were basically green and white, the owner's favorite colors for a garden, plus a little mauve and blue. Extensive use of dramatic green foliage plants, such as hosta, bergenia, artemisia, senecio, hebe, and variegated ivies adds architectural interest to the borders.

The far wall, originally planned as a woodland garden, remains as wild as possible, both to conceal neighbors' walls and to provide a dark backdrop to the green-and-white color scheme of the garden. Five original plane trees provide density, supplemented by generous plantings of philadelphus and other shrubs. The most recent addition, a gazebo, with wisteria already waiting in place to be trained over it, now gives the vista from the house its satisfying conclusion.

Opposite: *A corner of the first room of the garden, the grays and greens of the hosta,* stachys lanata, *and santolina lightened by a riot of crambe.*

Above: *The yew-lined path acting as axis between the two sections of the garden is decorated with climbing roses, iris, and* Alchemilla mollis.

A JEWEL OF A POOL

IN A LUSH SETTING

One of the major design challenges in making a garden today, particularly in a warm climate, is siting the swimming pool. An aerial view of Southern California, for instance, shows endless strings of angular or kidney-shaped pools, all in brilliant aquamarine hues, engulfing what is left of the landscape.

When author/actress/mother Suzy Carter bought this small Los Angeles ranch house in 1981, the garden, consisting of three-quarters of an acre, was almost entirely taken up by a swimming pool placed right outside the back door. The house was designed on a central axis with two small wings, allowing windows to look out into the backyard and

pool area, and beyond to the unappealing vista of a neighbor's high wall. "No one wanted to sit outside," says Suzy Carter. "There was no space for plants, there was no view from the windows, there was no overall concept for the space."

What was wrong was easy to see. To put it right was more complicated. Mrs. Carter must have interviewed at least 10 landscape architects in her search for help. "Nearly all of them said I must move the pool, which was economically impossible, or told me that the space was too disastrous to be worked on." In near despair, she agreed to meet with Denis Kurtz, senior vice president of Emmet L. Wemple & Associates, the firm responsible for the

Previous page: With the white pillars of the arbor reflected in the shimmering blue waters of the poolscape, there is a hint of classical Greece in this utterly contemporary setting.

Opposite: The pool is the unabashed center of this garden, with the house wrapping around on three sides and the arbor running along the fourth wall. Elegant brick trim enhances the sinuous rhythms of the glittering water.

Above: Leaving the pool, one ventures into very different country, with grass and rural stepping-stones.

Left: The high white wall conceals the neighbors' territory, covered in vines and a pleasing backdrop for admiring the view.

Above: *At the end of the stepping-stone path, a white lattice gateway leads the visitor into Suzy Carter's cymbidium garden.*

Top right: *The cymbidiums were planted to bloom as long as possible—from November through June—a treasure trove of greens, rusts, reds, pinks, whites, and yellows.*

Above center: Clematis jackmanii *adds its vibrant purple to the scene.*

Above right: *A white potato vine* (Solanum jasminoides) *cascades over the entrance to the cymbidium garden.*

landscaping of the Getty Museum in Los Angeles. His response was what she had been longing to hear —to work with what she had. "There were too many large elements," he recalls. "The pool and lower patio were disjointed from the house. The garden was also out of proportion to the scale of the house. It needed simplification and cohesiveness."

In this case, the position of the house was crucial, since it faced the pool and patio on three sides. The challenge was to make the house relate better to the pool without ripping out the pool, and to provide some kind of perspective and interest to the space beyond it. "In fact, we remodeled the pool," says Suzy Carter.

Mr. Kurtz redefined its perimeter by rounding all the hard edges and relining it with elegant brick edging. Curved steps were built down from the patio, making the deck area softer and the area around the pool more inviting. The hard edges of the beds on each side of the patio were reshaped and rounded, to acknowledge the geometry and proportions of the house. This rearrangement provided three seating areas around the pool, in spite of the small area of the patio.

There was no room to put in plants tall enough to disguise the neighbor's fence, so the landscape architect came up with the idea of an arbor. "Now we have the reflective qualities of the columnar arbor and a vine climbing over the top. By painting it white, we architecturally tied that side of the garden to the rest of the house." The arbor now provides that essential visual focus beyond the pool, giving a sense of space and light beneath the California sky, and also another place to sit and watch the setting sun.

The other major change was to remove all the planting along the bedroom wall, to the right of the patio, and put in a lawn. Softly rounded stepping-stones now make a charming rural path across the lawn, with mature citrus trees—orange, lemon, and

Top: Even in this tiny space, so dominated by water, there are three seating areas, each with equally magical views.

Above: In complete contrast to the formal feeling of the pool area, the country walk is lined with a tangle of fully grown citrus trees on one side and two Chinese magnolias on the other, offering shade, color, and subtle fragrance to the senses.

lime—on one side, and two Chinese magnolias on the other. Beneath them are shade plants such as azaleas, English ivy, violets, and forget-me-nots. This new area visually expanded the space into what feels like a woodland garden, providing a contrast from the bright-colored, open terrace to the darker vista beyond. And the reward at the far end of this walk? A white gateway into a small outdoor chamber for Mrs. Carter's cymbidium collection.

To decorate her new garden, Mrs. Carter, a passionate plantswoman, drew on her life's experience. "I love English gardens," she says, "but I lived in Hawaii a long time and have a strong Hawaiian heritage. My children were born there." Acknowledging both influences, she selected a large number of container plants for color and scent, including jasmine, gardenia, dianthus, nemesia, streptosolen, and gartenmeister fuchsia. As well as her cymbidiums, numerous specimen plants were also absorbed into the development of the design. "There was a magnolia tree growing in a rounded, raised planter that completely interrupted the movement of the garden," she recalls. "We moved it—with some trepidation, for magnolias are tricky to move—to add proportion and scale and protection from the afternoon sun." The tree also adds an element of visual depth between house and pool. Each different grouping of pots provides changing color with the seasons, a triumph of horticulture over climate.

For Suzy Carter, after wondering if she could ever find someone who would help her achieve what she wanted (a problem faced by many new garden owners), the results are truly satisfying. The spectacular plants speak for themselves in this redrawn, simplified garden, in which the pool, formerly an eyesore, now sits comfortably in its site, surrounded by graceful shapes and forms, and where visitors enjoy a pleasing vista from every window. "With Denis's help, we have done it," she says. "So my advice is 'Never give up!' "

Opposite and above: Mrs. Carter's collection of container plants changes with her whim and the seasons. Blue pansies, toadstool, lobelia, dusty-miller, dwarf stock, camellias, buttercup-yellow chrysanthemums, gardenmeister fuchsia, and marguerites are some of her favorites. The brightly colored plants in their pots seem an integral part of the overall design of the garden, a remarkable achievement.

GARDENS

When the eye is trained to perceive pictorial effect, it is
frequently struck by something—some combination of
grouping, lighting and colour—that is seen to have that
complete aspect of unity and beauty that to the artist's eye
forms a picture. Such are the impressions that the artist-
gardener endeavours to produce in every portion of the
garden.

Gertrude Jekyll (1843–1932)

RHETT
1954 – 1967
DEAR OL

WITH A PAST

A FAMOUS GARDEN DESIGNED

FOR POSTERITY

The idea of planting a garden for future generations may not concern most gardeners, but for the famous English *salonnière* and literary celebrity, Lady Ottoline Morrell, her garden was both her favorite creation and greatest legacy. Friend to D. H. Lawrence, Lytton Strachey, Aldous Huxley, Siegfried Sassoon, Virginia Woolf, Maynard Keynes, and most of the other literary and artistic figures of the day, Lady Ottoline Morrell drew them to her garden at Garsington Manor and provided them with a place to rest, to create, and sometimes, susceptible creatures, to fall in love. She fell in love a few times herself, and mostly rather unsuitably. But no one ever faulted her taste as a garden maker.

In 1925, she wrote in her diary, "If I leave here, I wonder what will happen to my lavender hedges and the Irish yews and the Italian cypresses, and the Ilex trees and avenues? I hope they will endure and be beautiful hundreds of years hence." She need not have worried. After several owners and over 60 years later, the gardens of Garsington Manor, near Oxford, remain one of the wonders of England.

The house dates from about 1570 and is built out of the soft Cotswold stone typical of the area. Dramatically situated at the top of a hill, with views all the way to the Berkshire Downs, the gardens radiate out on three sides, offering entirely different styles and vistas. Each flows into the next without any sense of discontinuity, and because of the per-

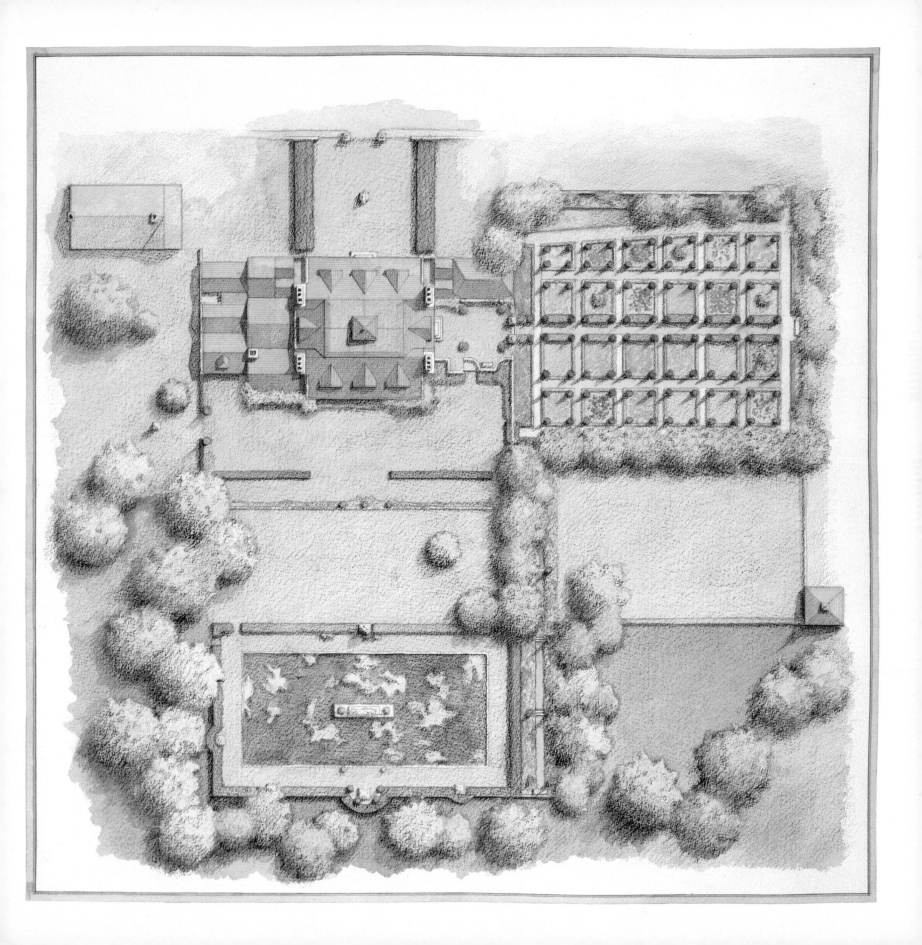

sistently steep gradient on which the gardens are laid out, the very act of entering and leaving each area provides a feeling of drama.

The most brilliant garden is the flower garden, to the east of the house, a walled enclosure divided into 24 square beds, each corner of which is planted with an Irish yew—which makes 96 yews! The beds, planted with a mixture of annuals and perennials, are divided by grass paths. This was the work of Lady Ottoline and her husband, Philip, always her chief supporter. "It was said that if the Morrells had to choose between adding a bathroom to their house or a statue to their garden they would choose the statue," Lord David Cecil wrote of them.

Stepping down from this formal space, one faces a large lawn that in Lady Ottoline's time was a tennis court, and is now used, amongst other things,

Previous page: The flower garden at Garsington—24 square beds, each corner of which is planted with an Irish yew sentinel, surrounded by seasonal annuals and perennials making 24 dazzling carpets of color.

Opposite: The east facade of the manor house, built of warm Cotswold stone, its towering chimneys typical of 16th-century English architecture.

Above: The front entrance to the house, facing north, with yew hedges on each side so high that they betray their age. They are more than 200 years old.

for the village play. Surrounding the lawn are borders of lavender, pinks, and roses, and at the far end is a very old dovecote with the date 1714 inscribed over the door. From this informal open space one then finds oneself deliciously enclosed again, in a series of high yew hedges that surround the formal pool in the Italian garden, sited at the bottom of the hill, facing the south side of the house. Some parts of this hedge are double-planted, making a secret walkway, and it is said that Lady Ottoline would walk along this yew *allée,* in some outlandish garb (for which she was famous), reading the poetry of Dryden aloud to the attending peacocks. The boathouse on the lake was taken from Lady Ottoline's earlier home, and her planting of ilexes leads the eye up the hill to the fine south facade of the house. Statues and a fountain add to the Italian flavor, as do glimpses of the dark irish yews soaring up over the walls of the flower garden to the east.

From this elegant and ornamental garden one moves west to a wild and woody area, with a natural pool fed by a spring, a stream garden, and a lime walk back to the house. Outside the west wall of the house is yet another garden, a tiny *potager* with a topiary hawthorn at its center.

Opposite: *The May blooming of white and purple tulips and forget-me-nots in all its glory. The tripods contain climbing roses.*

Above: *A seated Venus is poised comfortably atop rich cushions of aubretia.*

Left: *Brilliant color contrasts with old and mellowed stone— a constant theme in this garden.*

Above: The Juniper Walk—steps and grass, lined with blue and white bluebells, yellow lily-flowered tulips, and other spring bulbs. A cherry tree blooms up the slope, and in the distance are striking columns of yews in the flower garden.

Above right: The view through clouds of aubretia down the Juniper Walk, with a welcoming white garden seat at the far end.

Opposite: Through the flower garden looms one of the oldest dovecotes in England. It is inscribed 1714.

Overleaf: Lady Ottoline Morrell's lake, with Venus and a headless Cupid in the central platform and Vulcan guarding the rear. Beyond the double and triple rows of privet hedges stretches the glorious Oxfordshire countryside.

Lady Ottoline, who caught typhoid fever in Italy as a young woman, convalesced with her aunt at the Villa Capponi outside Florence, and it is thought her lifelong love affair with Italian gardens dates from that time. There is no doubt that Garsington owes a great debt to the Renaissance gardens of Italy, but its character is too varied to subscribe to an academic formula. Like its eccentric owner, the garden has many moods and inspired many emotions. ". . . Is the sunlight ever normal at Garsington?" wrote Virginia Woolf. "No, I think even the sky is done up in pale yellow silk, and certainly the cabbages are scented."

The Morrells were pacifists, and during the First World War, Garsington became a center for conscientious objectors, who helped on the farm. After the war, the Morrells' lives and fortunes changed, and in 1928 they were forced to sell their beautiful manor house and garden. At the auction, a large number of myrtle, lemon verbena, box, and laurel trees were offered for sale, indicating how Lady Ottoline's continuing plans for her Italian masterpiece had been sadly curtailed.

Happily the present owners, Mr. and Mrs. Leonard Ingrams, have respected their famous predecessors' passion, and their own planting, in particular around the sunken lawn and on the new front

lawn, has sustained the thread that ties the garden so powerfully to its past. As Humphrey Repton said, "All rational improvement of grounds is necessarily founded of a due attention to the character and situation of the place to be improved; the former teaches us what is advisable, the latter what is possible to be done." Some people may complain about inheriting a garden so uncompromisingly designed, preferring to create something entirely from scratch. In this case, the legacy is irresistible, and to be able to enjoy it, while enhancing its beauty, must surely be reward enough.

Opposite top: *The upper pond, fed by natural spring water, surrounded by sprinklings of spring bulbs.*

Opposite bottom: *This woodland on the west side of the garden intensifies the visual effect of the formality to the east.*

Right: *Lime trees, planted by Lady Ottoline Morrell, create a stylish* allée *lined with daffodils in the spring.*

Above: *A 20th-century classical garden figure, set off by yellow polyanthus hybrids.*

Right: *Daffodils line the path up the slope to the west side of the house, with some of the Morrells' statuary looking on.*

A JAPANESE THEME FOR AN
EVERGREEN GARDEN

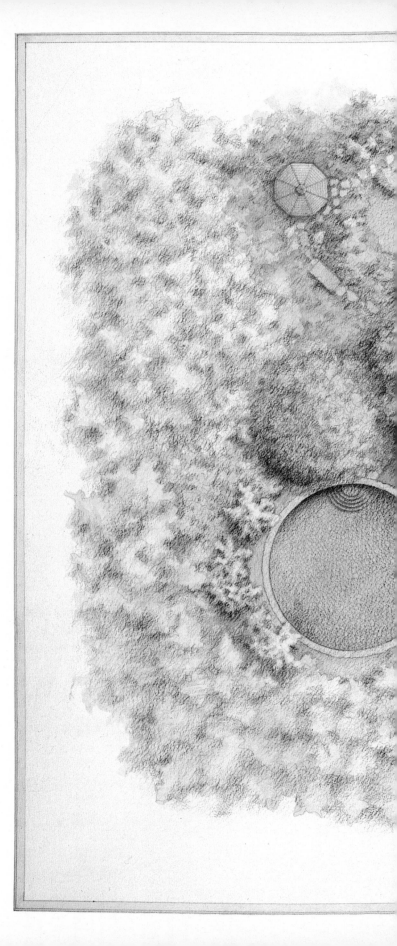

The house in Princeton, New Jersey, to which this garden belongs is historic. Woodrow Wilson lived here for two years when he was Governor of New Jersey and left it in 1913 to be inaugurated as President of the United States. Tudor in style, the house was designed at the turn of the century for artist Parker Mann, whose interest in Japanese architecture is apparent from the roofline and other details, an influence picked up and carried to an enthusiastic conclusion by its present owners, Dr. and Mrs. James M. Hester.

Dr. Hester grew up gardening but did not have time to fulfill his interest until his return from assignment in Japan, in 1980, and his assumption at that

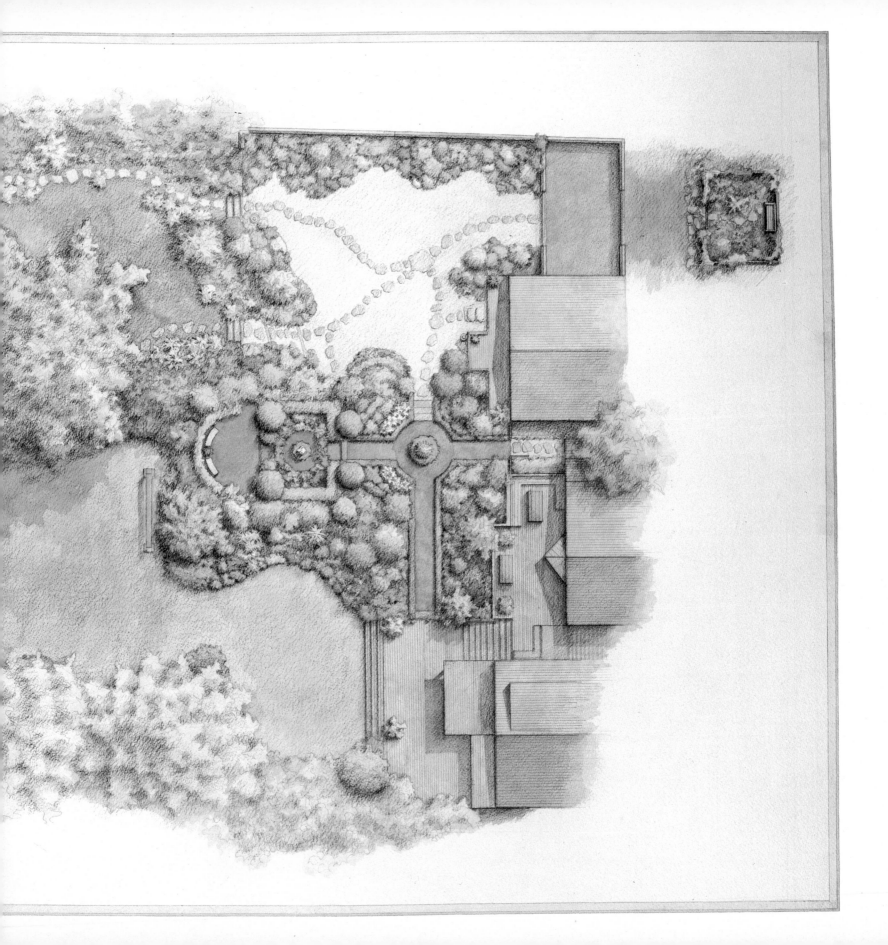

Opposite: From the far end of
the garden, a wooded vista
leads the eye up the slope to the
Hesters' Tudor-style house, its
half-timbered facade lending
itself to the Japanese elements
found in the landscape.

Left: Looking at the full length
of the back of the house from
the Japanese garden, showing
the extensive decks framing the
exterior, and allowing many
vantage points from which to
view the garden.

time of the presidency of the New York Botanical
Garden. "This seemed a wonderful opportunity to
live up to my new job," he says. "We knew we
wanted a Japanese garden, and I was able to draw
on the best talent right on my doorstep, Yuji Yoshimura, bonsai expert at the Botanical Garden." For
the other part of the garden the Hesters called on the
distinguished landscape architect Robert Zion. "We
wanted Bob to give us a self-contained environment,
evergreen, and low maintenance."

The garden of their Princeton house was at that
time a simple Victorian-style layout, with a red flagstone terrace and screened porch looking out on the
lawn, a small perennial border, dogwoods, other
shrubs, two large beech trees, and a small, brick-
paved "hidden garden" to the right of the main terrace. Robert Zion, of the well-known firm Zion &
Breen (recognized by New Yorkers for the wonderful little Paley Park), believes in the garden's being a
series of outdoor rooms, with the shrubs and flowers as furniture, trees as ceiling, the lawn as a rug to
carpet the floor. For the Hester garden, he carved
two beds of evergreens, mostly azaleas, laurel, and
rhododendrons, out of each side of the gently sloping lawn to make a narrow "doorway" down to a
circular pool at the bottom. The effect of this was to
create two self-contained spaces, or rooms, one near
the house, the other at a distance. The pool, a Zion

Right: The pool, 35 feet in diameter, 5½ feet deep at its deepest point, is a cool and serene focal point, fringed with bamboo, hollies, and rhododendrons.

Below: Known as an Old Charleston Joggling Board, this traditional rocking seat was first made as therapy for a lady with arthritis in Charleston, South Carolina.

masterpiece, is 35 feet in diameter, painted black, shimmering in summer and winter like a mysterious lake (although it is a working swimming pool). The far perimeter is framed in bamboo, hollies, and rhododendrons, a dense backdrop shutting out views of neighbors and evoking a feeling of privacy and serenity.

The excavations produced by digging out the pool were used to build a hill to the right of the pool, which was later topped with a gazebo, making a focal point for the view from the house. From the gazebo, the vista is like a woodland, with shade from massive beech trees and a floor of pachysandra

Above: *A view of the new arch, yet to be decorated with its flowers. High-rising white cleome adds drama to the entrance to this little garden.*

A garden within a garden— almost hidden by walls of ivy and spreading shrubs such as yew, weigela, chamaecyparis, and lilac. A small statue rises above the ivy to guard the brick paths, lined with beds filled with campanula, candytuft, dianthus, and annuals. Originally, this little "room" was open to the sky, but the Hesters have added an arch, up which will grow New Dawn roses and purple clematis.

and ferns (the fern planting copied from Winterthur), leading to the Japanese garden and back to the house. One of the beech trees recently died, and the space was filled with a weeping cherry. In the spring this wooded area is alive with Spanish bluebells, also an idea from Winterthur.

Meanwhile, Yuji Yoshimura was working his magic on the totally undeveloped part of the garden. The garage was redesigned as a teahouse/studio, with its own little deck, and a very plain Japanese-style wall was created to enclose the garden that Mr. Yoshimura made with local rocks, stones, and plants, and some of his own specially trained bonsai. Without a written plan, Mr. Yoshimura staked out and placed every rock and every shrub in this perfectly formed landscape. In its first incarnation, there was grass between this and the main garden. In time, large, whitish gravel stones replaced the grass, enhancing quite dramatically the range and intense color of the green shrubs.

Opposite: *The lily pond with pieris and evergreen shrubs.*

Top: *The Japanese garden, backed by a simple wall that reflects the architecture of the house.*

Above: *At first the stepping-stones were set into grass, but the plantings stood out better when contrasted with the neutral color of the gravel.*

Opposite: *From the Japanese garden, a path leads through the wooded area under the vast beech tree toward a simple gazebo. The weeping cherry is a new addition.*

Right: *In the vista from the gazebo toward the Japanese garden, a forest floor of ferns, pachysandra, and carpets of Spanish bluebells in the spring delight the eye.*

Walking past the back of the house and kitchen deck toward the large, open main deck (which replaced the red flagstone terrace and screened-in porch), one comes upon a tiny secret garden, with yuccas and ivy as an introduction to the circular enclosed space, lined with evergreens and a neat ilex hedge installed by Robert Zion. This year the Hesters added two English cottage arches, with roses and clematis being trained up them.

As with all passionate gardeners, the urge to improve did not stop there. "We thought a serious garden should have a good perennial bed," Dr. Hester says. "We had visited gardens in England and felt ours lacked that essential element." So he turned to perennial specialist Lynden Miller, restorer of the Conservatory Garden and Zoo in Central Park and the perennial garden at the New York Botanical Garden. She and her partner Pepe Maynard borrowed some of the area taken by the Zion shrubbery while adding more bedding space to create the deep perennial border that now lines one side of the vista down to the pool. The planting scheme remains in color throughout the summer, thanks to clever flower choices, well-manured soil, and full sun all day long. And at the front of the house, where a new garage had been planned, Dr. Hester instead designed a charming little enclosed garden that could be bestowed, like a flowering jewel box, as a gift to the tiniest backyard.

The Hesters are happy with the changes they have made. "We were lucky to have an old house with some good old-fashioned planting," Dr. Hester says. "But it didn't really belong to us until we started to change it. Now we have worked to make it ours, and we enjoy it all year long. Some gardens don't reveal themselves easily. We can sit on our deck and see the pool, the perennial border and the Japanese garden all at once. We get more pleasure from sitting here than from anything else about the house."

Opposite: *Gateway into a jewel box of green and white foliage, framed with trellis.*

Above: *Much nicer than a garage, for which this rectangular space was originally designated, is this unexpected garden in which the Hesters grow shade-loving hostas and white roses.*

Right: *An octagonal window reveals the restful dreaming space within.*

AMBITIOUS REPLANTING WITH A SENSE OF HISTORY

The house, as always, comes first. Belonging until the 1950s to the vicars of the parish of Beenham in southwest England, this house features late-Georgian architecture that reflects the serenity and prosperity of the period. Its view across the garden and over the fields to St. Mary's Church expresses the typically 18th-century English spirit of Man surveying his acres and professing himself satisfied in the eyes of God.

The present owners, Charles and Mary Keen, knew better than to tamper with this outlook. Yet the garden was both unsatisfactory and neglected. "We knew we must respect the feeling of the house when we redesigned the garden," says Mary Keen,

herself a garden designer and author of *The Garden Border Book.* The Keens dug new flower beds and added an herb garden, an orchard, and a vegetable garden decorated with a series of fruit and flower-covered arches. Throughout they chose plant materials that harmonize with the period feel of the landscape and that are, in Mary Keen's words, "quite ordinary and informal."

The present garden, consisting of approximately two acres wrapped around the house, was embarked upon nine years ago. Mary Keen did not draw up a master plan. When she designs a garden, she prefers to work from the ground up, so to speak, walking around the property and planning as she goes. Her first priority was to make a kitchen garden, for she loves to eat what she plants. (For a summer lunch she digs up new potatoes and cooks them fresh from the ground.) What is now the kitchen garden, with its paths and arches, was a chicken run. "We laid out the paths in the kitchen garden first and planted the yew hedge behind the swimming pool," she says. "We had no money, so it was all very slow."

The herb garden evolved as an eye-pleaser from the kitchen window. Although the space faces north, the herbs grow well enough, and the brick paving that was chosen seems to make the garden feel Mediterranean in atmosphere. Beyond the herb garden to the north was a shabby vegetable garden, which was taken out and replanted with standard fruit trees to make a charming orchard.

At the south side of the house, the garden opens up to splendid vistas of open landscape, and in the distance, the church. A huge magnolia that almost covered the terrace was destroyed by honey fungus and fell down—fortunately, as it turned out, from a design point of view, for the Keens could then design a border, build up the steep bank that runs to the ilex, and add three Irish yews "to make the terrace garden more self-contained." An even

Opposite: View from the back of St. Mary's Farm, showing the vegetable garden with its neat rows of cabbage, lettuce, beans, etc., and the colorful flower arches. To the extreme right, an unusually wide grassy path creates a vista the length of the garden.

Above: The herb garden—a north-facing garden that seems not to mind the climate, its plants spilling out enthusiastically onto the brick paths. The rose that makes such a buoyant showing is Rosa Mundi.

Overleaf: The north-facing herb garden is enhanced by Rosa Mundi rosebushes and warm paths of brick. Catmint spills out from the central terra-cotta pot.

Opposite top: *A colorful section of the kitchen garden, beds laden with peonies, poppies, iris, delphiniums, and penstemon, and in the background, a small gazebo.*

Opposite bottom left: *From the top of the kitchen garden, looking down toward the lawn on the south side, lavender and white shades predominate.*

Opposite bottom right: *New Dawn roses frame the entrance to the kitchen garden, with the clear pink of Mme Isaac Pereire adding color to the delicate scheme.*

Above left: *Herbs and flowers in a collection of terra-cotta pots may be moved about according to the needs of the gardener and the garden.*

Above right: *A corner of the conservatory outside the kitchen, where a specially built brick wall encloses a drain, on which an old copper boiler now stands, planted with a climbing mignonette.*

Below right: *Clematis hybrid lines one side of the path leading to the gazebo.*

newer addition is a flight of steps leading up from the lower lawn to the terrace, balancing the steps that lead down from the south side of the house.

Looking out toward the large lawn and fields beyond, Mary Keen wanted more variety and interest, so she carved new beds out of the garden near the "Vicar's Walk" (a box hedge and path running down the side of the property to the church) and planted them with wild roses, geraniums, and foliage plants. The peninsulalike shape of the first bed provides a secret garden behind, where one may linger undisturbed. "I like the idea of people sitting in places where they can't be seen," she says. "I can never find anyone in this garden. I spend hours calling the family in to meals."

Mary Keen, like all passionate gardeners, is full of likes and dislikes. She loves enclosed gardens, but in this case the sweep of the landscape dictated her layout. She loves moving from a space filled with lots of bright sun and color into a dark shrubbery. "I like each area to be and feel different." Expressing an aversion to pinched, narrow paths, she believes a garden should be made to walk through. She has a very set walk around her garden, which she has carefully planned for herself. "You need to think how you walk around your garden," she urges. "I always go down the steps, for instance, not up." She asks

Top left: *English gardeners like the idea of decorating arches with fruit (here with pears) as well as with the more traditional roses.*

Top right: *The very deep, typically English border along the south side of the kitchen garden runs into a hedge, a gate, and green pastures beyond.*

Above left: *The bank has always been there, but the steps are new, as are the Irish yews, planted to give definition to the upper level of the garden.*

Above right: *The terrace garden at the southwest corner of the house, planted with white roses, mullein, cistus, Salvia turkestanica, nonflowering lambs' ears, winter jasmine up the wall, and, along the south border, bushes of rosemary.*

questions all the time as she walks. "Where the yew house now stands there was a rockery and a weeping willow. Should we replant another tree there? Trees take time. Might we use a mature tree to fill in? Can we afford it?"

The constant evolution of this garden is one of its charms. History is always in the making. "The point about this garden is that it is quite complicated and ambitious," she admits. "Yet for the first five years we had no help at all. People shouldn't be put off making an elaborate garden. You can have a wonderful garden without full-time gardeners. You

Window view of the south side of the garden looking out toward the perfectly framed focal point of St. Mary's Church.

A shady woodland path leads to a more untamed part of the garden.

Opposite, clockwise from top: *The swimming pool, carefully concealed from the main part of the garden, has been heavily planted with variegated dogwood; swimmers enjoy a fine view of the church.*

At the back of this secluded seating area is the "Vicar's Walk," which used to take the Reverend to and from church.

A shady place to plan one's garden.

A hammock offers rest after too much gardening.

These beech hedges are being encouraged to grow even higher to dramatize the allée to the far end of the garden.

simply have to be relaxed about maintenance. I'd like my garden to be twenty percent tidier." She shrugs. She uses the same plants that she knows will grow and not give trouble. When she makes her beds, she starts planting from the middle and works outward, to avoid weeding. The daisies on the lawn are intentional. "A garden is more than three-dimensional," she says, summing up. "It must feel comfortable as well as look nice."

FROM FARMLAND TO GARDEN IN

FOUR DECADES

The countryside from which this garden evolved is the agricultural land of central New Jersey. The house is an 18th-century farmhouse, gradually added to and extended over the years. Its appearance now has the flavor of a Southern plantation, with its Greek Revival portico and huge shade trees. The garden, covering about five acres and surrounding the house on all four sides, has both grand and informal aspects, offering a variety of views and moods to the visitor.

Its design originally came from the same impetus as most garden designs—a desire to have somewhere pleasing to sit directly outside the house. When the owners came to the garden during the Second World War, small brick terraces on the west and north sides of the house, with easy access from the house, filled this purpose. There was a second, lower cobblestone terrace on the north surrounded by box, attractive to look down upon, though not easy to reach. These, plus a crab apple orchard across the driveway from the house (where the barn originally stood), constituted the garden until after the war, when a much more ambitious gardening scheme was embarked upon.

Under the youthful but meticulous eye of head gardener George Knapp, who came to the garden in 1946, the west terrace was the first area of concentration. "I designed the extension of the terrace," George Knapp says. "It all fell away in a grassy slope

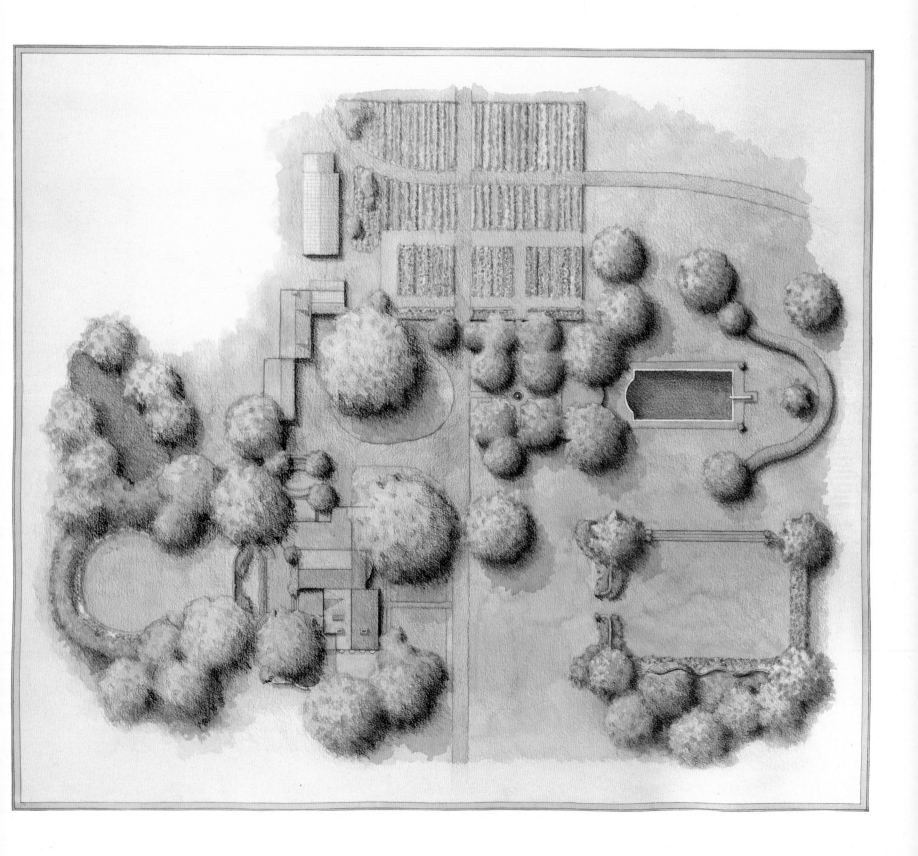

Opposite: Standing on the west terrace, one looks past the dappled shade to the fine Greek Revival portico of this expanded farmhouse.

Left: From the terrace there are vistas on all sides, with a hint of the surrounding farmland in the distance.

Above: The delicate architecture of the house is reflected in the graceful wrought-iron table and flower arrangement—creating an outdoor room.

before. There was a small elm growing here, and when the terrace went in, we debated whether to remove the tree or not. We made a nine-foot well of rock for it, and it thrived—thrived so much that one day it will push the wall over. Underneath there is nothing but roots."

The terrace was given a three-foot-high, curved, open-brick balustrade. At the end, a small pool, with the Shakespeare fountain (a working model of Ward's statue in New York's Central Park), is circled by a flower bed. On the side toward the driveway, a retaining wall was designed with niches in the bricks filled with pots of ivies and white begonias.

To the north, a semicircular garden was built below the terrace, with a path between, giving a

Above: *A statue of Shakespeare looks over the open-brick curved balustrade backing a small pool, with annual plantings (white mostly, petunias or begonias).*

From the end of the north terrace, near the Shakespeare statue, the garden falls away steeply on the left to the Circle Garden.

Architectural differences in window treatments indicate the changes this farmhouse has undergone since its 18th-century origins.

Right: *A shady path runs below the balustrade of the Shakespeare Garden toward an evergreen shrubbery and woods.*

sense of height to the face of the slope. This new garden was framed with a holly hedge, beyond which one can see the fields, dotted with Dorset sheep. Landscape architects Melva Weber and Alfred Geiffert helped George Knapp plan this part of the garden.

To the right of the semicircular garden, a pond was made by damming up an old creek. A little stream meanders west, its banks planted with hemlock, Japanese iris, and other shrubs. Later Mr. Knapp added a bridge, decorated with euonymus, and a series of new dams along the brook, with a

Opposite: The view from the Circle Garden shows the terracing effect of the slope from the house, densely planted with box and yew.

Above left: The Circle Garden is actually a semicircle, framed by a low wall and a holly hedge, over which the sheep pasture rises toward the horizon.

Top: When the bust of Oscar Wilde was brought by the owners into the Circle Garden, the wall was heightened to adjust the proportion.

Above: The pond was created out of a naturally formed gully, with Norway spruce giving height and shade. Shrubs, hemlock, Japanese iris, and an arrangement of rocks enhanced the natural feel of this part of the garden.

Left: *The arched entrance to the newest space—the Bear Garden—offers a vista of brick and gravel, with fine marble finials from Italy.*

Above: *A dappled path snakes around the house's latest addition of the library toward the Bear Garden.*

Opposite left: *Across the driveway is the small crabapple garden, consisting of two converging brick walks with a small fountain. At the far end of this path the glass doors of the swimming pool pavilion may be glimpsed.*

Opposite top right: *The crosswalk of the crabapple garden leads past the statue of Neptune toward a gate into the cutting garden. Annual plantings around the central fountain include spring bulbs and marigolds, with daisies and begonias in the summer.*

Below: *View of the front of the house across the driveway, with stone pelicans guarding the entrance to the garden and orchard.*

Bottom: *Looking into the walled garden, the visitor enjoys a large mixed border. The wall curves in the manner of one built at Monticello, and is anchored at the four corners by pin oaks.*

spring at the bottom, giving a charming rural aspect to this part of the garden. "If there is a nighttime party, I sometimes fill the reservoir higher up the hill and guests can hear the water cascading down. It makes a nice effect," he says.

One of the design challenges of this property was the position of the driveway, which bisects the landscape into two discrete areas. In this case there was nothing for it but to divide the landscaping accordingly. So one walks across the driveway to another series of gardens—the walled garden, the pool pavilion garden, and the crab apple garden. The walled garden is entered by a narrow space marked with two brick pillars, on an axis with the front door of the house. This intriguing entryway then opens up dramatically to a long mixed border on the right, and a vista left sloping down toward the swimming pool. The pool, added in the fifties, is most unusually placed in an orchard, so instead of the fenced-in feeling of most pools, here the bathers get a sense of swimming in open country. Through the pavilion is a vista of the crab apple garden, with its Italianate circular center and statue of Neptune (a detail in miniature of the famous fountain in Naples).

Although the two garden areas are divided by the driveway, they are unified by the vegetable and

Right: The vegetable and cutting garden, which links the house and the pool garden, planted with an astonishing display of herbs, vegetables, and colorful annuals.

Far right: Another view of the cutting garden, showing the beautiful old greenhouse with its curving eaves. Beyond the post and rail fence that contains this magnificent utility garden is the valley of the Raritan river.

(See Appendix for plant list.)

cutting garden, which traverses the whole distance between the south side of the house and the pool garden, with the line of the driveway acting as an axis leading down to a post-and-rail fence and beyond it, the cow pasture and the north branch of the Raritan River. Reckoning it covers at least one and a half acres, George Knapp calls this the utility garden, and the thousands of cuttings of mums, daisies, astilbe, sweet William, rudbeckia, ageratum, and lettuce, cabbage, beans, and other vegetables provide wonderful gifts, not only for the house, but also for the North Branch Church, the Fire Department, the Veterans Hospital, graduations, parties, and lucky visitors. "The greenhouse is always full," says George Knapp, and adds, "You have to be a little crazy. We work from dawn to dark."

The newest garden in this variety-filled landscape is the bear garden, so-called after the bear fountain by Wheeler Williams, which is set against the brick wall of the small and shady space. This garden was the result of a new library wing, which was added to the house. The view from its large east window, formerly looking straight out at a toolshed, now includes espaliered apple trees against a brick wall, a sunken oval of white granite pebbles beneath, and a raised border planted with myrtle and seasonal bulbs, including autumn crocuses.

Pools, Streams, and Fountains

Water is one of the most satisfying elements to be found in the garden. As well as its reflective qualities, water offers feelings of serenity, fruitfulness, and the soothing sounds that harmonize with the other pleasing sounds of the garden. All the most famous gardens have some water in them, whether it is simply a small round pond surrounded by high hedges, as at Hidcote, or a dramatic torrent of water tumbling down a steep incline, as at the Villa Caprarola.

Needless to say, irrigation, filters, and drainage are all considerations the garden designer must resolve satisfactorily before embarking on a pool, canal, or waterfall. Small fountains can be fitted out with pumps. Cascades can be homemade with a length of hose, a pump, and some strategically placed rocks. The market for these devices is growing. The only foreseeable problem is ecological and planetary. How long will there be enough water to go around? Fears of drought are accentuated by recent summers in the United States. Will English rain diminish? As we admire our lovely fountains, we fervently hope not.

THE GARDEN AS PERSONAL
BIOGRAPHY, FULL OF WIT AND DRAMA

Sir Roy Strong has left a lasting impression on British culture, first as head of the National Portrait Gallery, and most recently as director of the Victoria and Albert Museum. But perhaps his most abiding legacy will concern neither art galleries nor museums, although both richly contribute to it, for in the last 15 years Sir Roy and his wife, the distinguished theatrical designer Julia Trevelyan Oman, have created what may be the largest formal garden made in England since 1945.

The Strongs' country house had a modest garden and a field with cows grazing on it—a little over three acres in all. With this landscape, in 1974, Sir Roy launched the first earthworks for what was to become a series of "rooms" flowing into each other, bound by a sense of symmetry, architecture, and subtle color schemes, reflecting the unwavering vision of the architect, and marked by personal references that serve as a kind of horticultural autobiography.

It is an astonishing achievement, inspired largely by the images found in his book *The Renaissance Garden in England.* "I began to get hooked on these engravings of seventeenth-century English gardens," he recalls. "I thought, Why can't I do that?" His house made no objection. Simple in design, it looks out across a small lawn to a large cedar tree and the countryside beyond. There is a terrace, decorated with herbs, sedums, and geraniums in pots

This page, clockwise from top: A cedar tree, with an underplanting of bulbs and a glimpse of the Herefordshire countryside, betrays little of the design virtuosity of the rest of the garden.

A hint of the formal style adopted by Sir Roy Strong, viewed from the house.

Pink hyacinths add color to an urn garden with a tree seat in the background.

A vista of beech hedges and a grassy walk.

Opposite, clockwise from top left: Modest gate and driveway to a visionary landscape.

Statues adorn the garden more prominently than flowers.

A yew allée "closed" by an obelisk.

This lion was rescued from the House of Commons.

Topiary and a beech hedge lead the eye to a pinnacle from All Souls, Oxford.

(his wife's domain), and an old summerhouse used to winter over tender plants. To this landscape Sir Roy added the Yew Garden, with a lion from the Houses of Parliament as a focal point, Torte's Garden, named after one of the family cats, the Lady Torte de Shell, and the Fledermaus Walk, an *allée* lined with a beech hedge, punctuated by a pinnacle originally from All Souls College, Oxford.

This garden is satisfying in itself, but it hardly begins to prepare the visitor for what lies ahead. Crossing the driveway, one enters an intensely personal world of gardening history, fantasy, humor, and consummate elegance, all carved out of one flat field.

Sir Roy freely admits that he is a garden designer rather than a plantsman. His wife's knowledge of and fascination with plants invariably complements the formality of the various layouts. His approach to gardening is that of a set designer,

Opposite top: *The Serpentine Walk winding its way through spring bulbs.*

Opposite center: *The Ashton Arbour, a favorite resting place.*

Opposite bottom: *A noble bust guards the Arbour.*

Right: *Sir Roy Strong's 50th Birthday Garden, a formal patio in brick and stone designed by his wife, leading to the Shakespeare Monument, a prize awarded to Sir Roy for his services to the Arts.*

seeing the garden as a stage, or a series of theatrical backdrops, with the visitor as audience, invited to enjoy the drama. Hence each little "stage" is totally different in style and mood. The 1977 Jubilee Garden (named for the Queen's Silver Jubilee), for instance, is essentially green and white with shades of purple, lilac, and mauve, laid out in a long, open vista down a paved walk to a roundel dominated by a sundial that once belonged to Cecil Beaton. The Pierpont Morgan Rose Garden (realized thanks to the library's fee to Sir Roy for a series of lectures) is enclosed by high yew hedges and defined by formal edging to the rose beds. The Scandinavian Grove is a shady woodland with primroses, cowslips, and hellebores. The Ashton Arbour (aptly named for the late Sir Frederick Ashton, a frequent colleague of Julia Trevelyan Oman) has a seat from which one may survey a carefully staged vista through to the orchard—and so on.

The gardens are added step by step, like markers in their owners' lives, as time and money allow. (The newest one is a salute to Sir Roy's term of office at the Victoria and Albert Museum.) No big budget here, in spite of appearances. Contrary to the overpowering impression of grandeur offered by the clipped hedges, topiary, and plantings, the garden requires low maintenance. Although looking authentically ancient, many of the statues come from dealers or catalogs. There are few bedding flowers, no elaborate perennial borders, no needy container plants. Two helpers clip the hedges and mow once or twice a fortnight, and Sir Roy himself does all the topiary. His philosophy is uncompromising on this score: "I'd rather have a grand spectacle roughly kept than everything trimmed with nail scissors." This thesis depends on strong "bones" in a garden, a firm architectural sense, and sculpture to anchor a vista and create a focal point. These were the guidelines used in many Dutch, Italian, and English Renaissance garden designs, to which the Strong

Opposite: *The Pierpont Morgan Rose Garden, decorated with box edging, a variety of scented old roses such as Rosa Complicata, Honorine de Brabant, Souvenir de la Malmaison, Albéric Barbier, Mme. Hardy, Blanc Double de Coubert, and standard amelanchiers for height.*

Above: *The central feature of the Rose Garden is an urn given to Julia Trevelyan Oman by her aunt, author Carola Oman, encircled by nepeta, santolina, spring tulips, and summer salvia.*

garden owes such a handsome debt.

Few people today would have the courage, let alone the vision, to embark on a garden as brilliant and ambitious as this one. Sir Roy's friends, such as the late John Fowler and Cecil Beaton, inspired him. His career with art and art objects refined his eye. His wife's artistic imagination enhanced the garden's form. "It's very personal and rather dotty," concedes Sir Roy. "But I don't see why anyone couldn't do something like this. You don't have to have everything done at once. Capital outlay on statues and so forth has to occur when it can be afforded. The thing is to get the hedges and trees to make the setting for them. I was so broke in 1974 that all I could put in the middle of one rose garden was a rockery of stones found here!"

It is marvelously encouraging to realize that all of this garden was made out of a blank field in *fourteen years.* "People don't believe that a yew hedge will grow this big in their lifetime. But I saw it all as soon as I put it in. All the design is done by eye. No mathematics." And yet in spite of this prodigious effort, Sir Roy assures the fainthearted that one should be relaxed about gardening. "If you fail to prune a shrub at exactly the right time it will probably not be disastrous," he wrote in his book *Creating Small Gardens.* "Once a garden becomes a burden, it ceases to be a pleasure."

The pleasure Roy Strong derives from his garden is almost tangible. "It's a garden full of friends," he says. "Plants are given us by other gardeners, by relations, passed on from our grandparents' generation. Everywhere we look are reminders of our lives. That's a wonderful feeling." One of his favorite places to sit is in the Ashton Arbour, surrounded by vistas and suffused with the presence of old friends. "It gives me a feeling of peace and privacy," he says. "Our whole life is in this garden."

Opposite: *The reverse view of the Rose Garden, the eye being led upward to the distant obelisk.*

Above: *Cecil Beaton's armillary dominates a planting of English cottage flowers—foxgloves, lupines, roses, campanula.*

Left: *This stunning vista of the Jubilee Garden was created entirely by eye, not mathematics, out of a piece of cow pasture.*

Left: *At the end of the Christmas Orchard, one of Sir Roy Strong's many classical sculptural ornaments observes a carpet of daffodils.*

Right: *One of the many varieties of* allée *created by the designer, this one offers rows of pleached limes underplanted with hundreds of daffodils, leading to a covered Gothic-inspired seat.*

GARDENS IN

Out of doors you may have a building or a tree which is a fixed point you have to accept. Such an object or even a group of objects produces a specific vibration, which may require subduing or reinforcing; and so, aware of this factor, you start composing by adding or subtracting shapes and textures and using colours and tones to achieve the impression you want to make.

Russell Page (1906–85)

THE LANDSCAPE

BRUSH STROKES
IN A LANDSCAPE

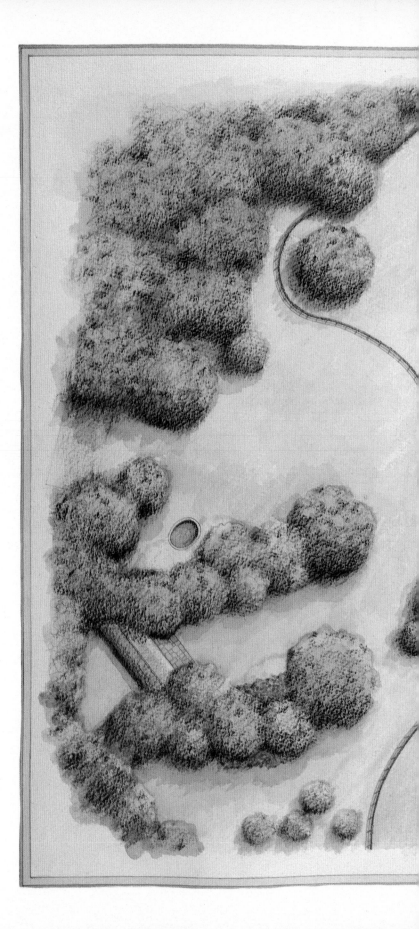

In all the history of garden design, one theme remains constant—the dynamic relationship between Man and Nature. From the earliest religious gardens made by monks and nuns to the great 18th-century English parklands, from the symbolic landscapes of China to the formal *parterres* of the royal French palaces, from herbs to roses, medicinal plants to specimen trees, it has always been the same—the struggle to achieve a balance between the will of Man and the power of Nature. The 18th-century English garden maker Humphry Repton offered a felicitous definition of his profession in his 1816 book on the subject: "The whole art of landscape gardening may properly be defined as the pleasing combination of art and na-

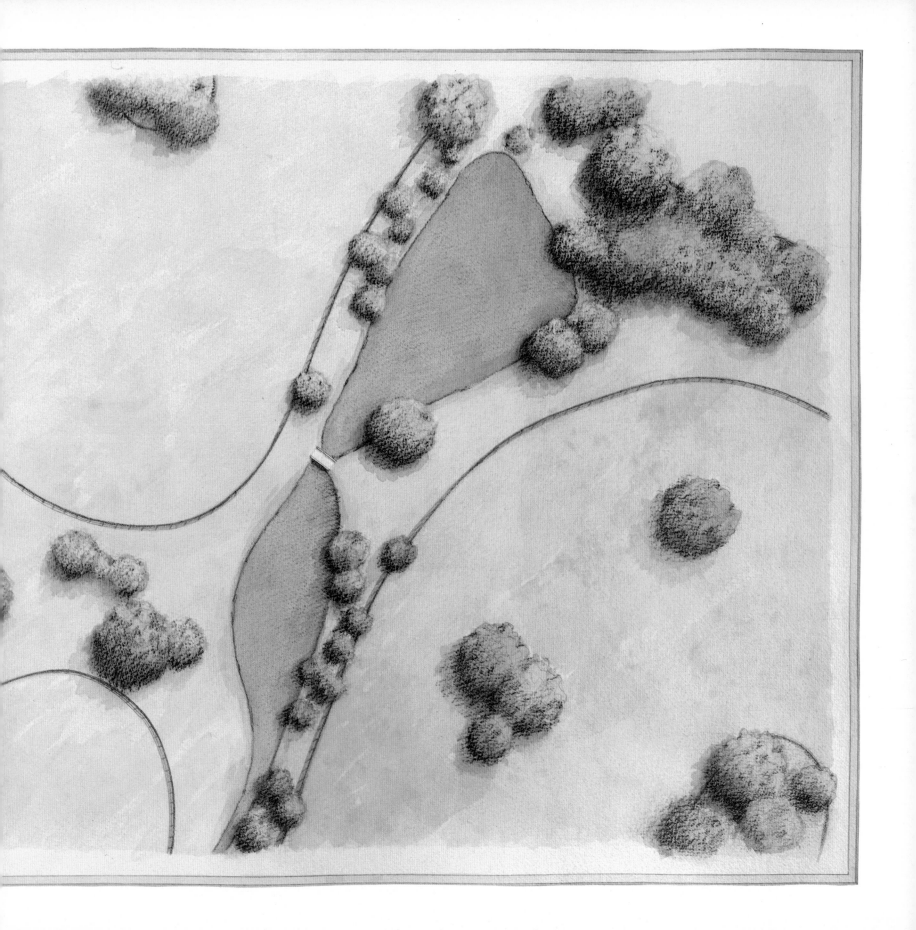

ture adapted to the use of Man."

This 1,600-acre horse farm in Kentucky presents perhaps the ultimate challenge to the designer, the greatest test of his art, the most dramatic example of how Man may work with Nature in ways the backyard gardener may not yet have contemplated. Landscape architect Morgan Wheelock, asked to turn over a thousand acres of farmland into a horse farm, with barns, paddocks, and exercise areas, plus a domestic garden for the 19th-century farmhouse, was perfectly aware of the complexity of his task and of the role he must play.

"Landscape architecture as an art form is totally different from architecture or sculpture. In the latter two, the practitioner is in control of everything. A landscape architect is simply a moderator or orchestra leader in the hands of Mother Nature."

Mr. Wheelock has been designing gardens for many years and has come to see his work as expressive of much more than merely the placement of trees or the alignment of paths. "My goal is to try to reveal the essence of the land in the abstract. I'm not creating a knot garden or a cottage garden or any kind of garden per se. What I am trying to do is, one, formulate a marriage between the land as it is and what its potential is; two, establish what the land is to be—farm, corporate headquarters, and so forth; three, divine the aspirations and dreams of the individual who owns the land, how he may express himself through the land; and four, act as a catalyst or channel in this whole process to connect the material and spiritual motivations of the individual with the realities inherent in the character of the land."

In working on this Kentucky horse farm, Mr. Wheelock was led to the most extreme test of these requirements, for in this case he was attempting to express something far more than a modest garden plot. He was being asked to lay out grid lines, hedgerows, fences, barns, paths, hills, plateaux, a monumental landscape such as Capability Brown

Previous page: Almost Japanese in their fluid lines, the fences of this horse farm snake their way across the vast pastures.

Opposite: The garden near the house is as blowsy as the surrounding landscape is restrained, with columbine, fritillaria, astilbe, delphinium, and salvia.

Top: Container plants decorate a shallow flight of steps.

Above: Brick as decoration— the hint of a Moon Gate surrounded by ivy.

A shady woodland path near the house was formed from old stones saved from digging out the garden.

Right: *The pool was sited over a sinkhole—a geological characteristic of Kentucky where the land dips to form a hole. The hole is formed in soluble rock by the action of water.*

Water relieves the flat plains of the former cattle fields while lush shade trees temper the summer heat.

might have dreamed of, and yet maintain a consistent sense of where he stood in the eternal balancing act between Man and Nature.

"You must study the land. Learn what it wants to be, before you make any move. I visualize, step aside out of my own ego, and let images come in. I tune into the scale, the size, the heat, the cold, the friendliness, the hostility, the light, the dark. I see the whole design before I begin to draw. Then I go back to the land and ask again, till I am sure."

It sounds mystical, but then it probably is. "The forces of Nature are always greater than the forces of man's ego. You dare to change the land? You are playing co-creator with God. That is enough to make anyone mystical."

In planning every line, every curve of the fences that snake their way across what were once cattle fields (he saw the black-painted fences as brush strokes on the landscape), Mr. Wheelock and his colleagues drove a car up and down the grassy fields, leaving track marks, like big fingers tracing lines that would ultimately become the fences. Nothing mystical about that. Nothing mystical either about the earth moving, which was required to grade the gently undulating hills and valleys, nor about the planting. Almost every tree on the property—huckleberries, pears, sweet gums, evergreens—was dropped in place to complement the landscape.

"In Nature, nothing is static. What is small today will be large tomorrow. When a white pine is young, it looks like a little Christmas tree; when it is old, it looks like an oak. You must anticipate the movement of Nature."

As well as taking on this vast project, Morgan Wheelock was also asked to make a garden to surround the 19th-century brick farmhouse that is the focus of this terrain. Here again, the land itself dictated much of the design. The curved walls around the pool, the woody slope leading up to the house,

the raised terrace, all reflect the landscape. Informal herbaceous planting, almost wild in its abundance, contrasts with the meticulous, graceful lines of the fences that glide sinuously into the distance.

This is landscaping in its ultimate expression—hundreds of acres molded both to their own and to their owners' will. Its success rests with the viewer. "We are trying to achieve a balance—a kind of classicism if you like—between the romantic and the spiritual, the ecological and the scientific. We are looking for that extra dimension."

Every fence, every tree— hackberries, pears, sweet gums —meticulously positioned and planted to complement the landscape, creating an almost abstract vision of rhythm, movement, and serenity.

STATUARY IN THE MIDST OF
CLASSIC ENGLISH SCENERY

The unique charm of this garden is that it lies along the banks of the River Thames and is watched over by the Victorian Gothic spire of the village church, so that the given landscape adds a romantic dimension to the lawns, flowers, and statuary that abound here. The owner is antiques dealer Christopher Gibbs, who inherited the house and garden from his parents after it was spurned by his elder brothers. An ancestor designed the garden in the 1840s, making the most of the view by cutting a long path on the rocky shelf above the river, and enhancing it by replacing an ancient ferry with a six-arched Gothic bridge across the water. Now the garden is in the hands of an equally ambitious gardener.

"I am the sixth generation of my family to tend this garden, which occupies a long, thin site, sandwiched between a road and the river. Few features of the original planting remain. The ranks of tall elms which enclosed the garden succumbed to disease ten years ago, but at the church end stands a cedar of Lebanon brought back by Great Uncle John in 1864, shading a terrace of ivy and *Hydrangea petiolaris.*" A lawn stretches eastward around the south front of the house, broken by a square, hornbeam-hedged enclosure, planted for evening scent. Steps to a lower level lead one past painted statues of 18th-century generals to a grassy sward centered by a weeping lime with a circular iron seat.

Some of Christopher Gibbs's own contributions, culled from his work as a dealer in antiquities, include a painted stone cow browsing among the flowers, rescued from a Dublin dairy. Other interesting and sometimes eccentric statuary is placed at strategic points in the landscape. A broad gravel path with pots of agapanthus passes along the front of the house to a vast cube of clipped yew, 30 feet high. (The height and girth of a yew can date a garden as clearly as the rings on a tree trunk.) This fronts a large rose pergola, which bisects the garden on a north-south axis. A big mirror is placed beyond its northern end, reflecting to infinity a shady tunnel underplanted in autumn with blue crocuses and leading down by steep steps to the river.

"Beyond this tunnel lies the heart of the garden, with the main axis extending eastward under a rose-

Left: *The iris border in May, set against the side of the lime tunnel looking south.*

Above: *Rose-covered arch with spring plantings.*

covered trellis, flanked by double borders and backed with more trellis covered in roses and honeysuckle. This was my mother's creation. The outer borders are heightened by wedges of taller shrubs and roses, including a golden currant, buddleias, ceanothus, and Siberian lilac. Throughout the seasons the area is a glorious rainbow of continuing color and fragrance, and that's the way I like it."

Passing through this colorful border area, we enter the cool shade of the lime tunnel. In the spring it is a sea of pale blue grape hyacinth, giving way to little cyclamen. On the other side, a border of lilies of the valley mirrors the yellow irises. The vista is closed to the north by a heroic, marble, Roman head on draped stone shoulders which faces, at the other end, an old medlar tree set in a field of Regal lilies.

"To reach the orchard one must turn right into a little meadow, or Burne-Jones garden, as my aunts called it, seasonally interesting with bulbs in spring, white marble-berried *Sorbus hupehensis* in autumn,

Above left: From the lead generals' point of view, the river seems small when seen in the context of the water meadows and famous Wittenham Clumps of Oxfordshire.

Top: An 18th-century statue of Bacchus stands soberly in the orchard.

Above: A painted cow, rescued from a Dublin dairy, turns away in disdain from the rose pergola.

Left: Bacchus enjoys the view, whatever the season.

A glimpse of the Gothic bridge built by Christopher Gibbs's 19th-century ancestor to enhance the river and garden landscape, framed by pink chestnut blossoms and a backcloth of willows.

and *Prunus autumnalis* in winter." Beyond in the grass are old apple and pear trees, and in the midst of them a gaily painted 18th-century lead figure of Bacchus, which looks down a red-tinted grove to the curve of the river and its pollarded willows. This grove, newly planted by Mr. Gibbs, derives its color from copper beeches and purple hazels interspersed with *Prunus pissardii.* In years to come, he envisages a tawny tulip tree adding its flame color to this cheerful little wood.

From the orchard and extended groves alongside the riverbank, one turns down toward the water, where there are double paths shaded by tall trees and underplanted with many varieties of snowdrops and violets. This wilder, shadier world is knit

to the garden by steps at several points, and there are views cut out across the river to the meadows and hills beyond. Much of this land on the other side of the river is also owned by Mr. Gibbs, offering him the opportunity to become a modern Capability Brown, carving out vast swaths of distant landscape with clumps of trees and valleys and lakes. "I love borrowed scenery," he admits. "I plan all sorts of vistas across the river."

Though the garden is wonderful, it is not easy to work in. There are no longer foresters to trim the big trees, and the death of the elms has reduced the shade and played havoc with the subtle underplanting. The river walks are untidy and spotty. In gaps, Mr. Gibbs has planted white- and pink-berried cotoneasters and black-lipped or scarlet-thorned roses,

but it will take a long time before they frame the views into the countryside. Yet he has extremely ambitious plans for adding to the garden. "I haven't even begun the new plantings of oaks and swamp cypresses on the other bank of the river, where I plan a short, tapering-to-trick-the-eye avenue with a mysterious, druidish earthwork on which to seed cowslip and anemone pulsatilla. My plan for a fishing temple above my wild wood is still a dream, and although I march my tolerant friends along my circuit walk, pointing out the beauties, I can see by their glazed eyes and dazed expressions that I have a lifetime's task ahead. My dialogue with the *genius loci* has only just begun."

Top right: *The antiques dealer's storehouse is also his greenhouse, guarded by two 17th-century Roman emperors.*

Far right: *A marble baby naps on a bed of bluebells and pheasant's eye.*

Bottom right: *An arched walk with sculpture as focal point.*

Statuary

Classical gardens, and in particular those of the Italian Renaissance, depended heavily upon the use of statuary. These figures, often made by the greatest artists of the time, represented allegories relating to the garden or to the patrons of the garden, or invoked mythological creatures that would enhance the symbolic meanings of the garden. The statue of the flying horse Pegasus in the great fountain at the entry to the Villa Lante, for instance, refers to Parnassus—the gods' sacred garden—as indication of what the visitor to the garden may expect within the walls.

Today, landscape architects tend to be more wary of prescribing these props. Yet the strategically placed bust, urn, column, sundial, or other pleasing object fulfills the essential function of providing a focal point, or "closing" a vista. While it is difficult these days to find an original work of sculpture, modern reproductions are often very good. Sir Roy Strong's garden is peopled with fine statues obtained from catalogs and should encourage the timid to do the same.

Furniture

While statuary gives the garden a noble aspect, furniture provides a much more practical service. A carefully placed chair, bench, or simple seating arrangement offers a welcome respite for the weary weeder and a happy haven for meditation or enjoyment of the view. Stone, wrought iron, aluminum, and wood are some of the materials readily available for garden furniture. Old pieces are hard to come by, but garden designers are taking up the challenge. Barnsley House and Chatsworth are two famous country houses now producing their own line of furniture, for instance, and reproductions of the famous Lutyens bench are now almost a cliché.

Of course, applied with too much enthusiasm, furniture may lead the visitor to suppose he has wandered into an architectural salvage repository, or into some kind of outdoor café, with chairs and tables everywhere. Applied with too little conviction, the effect is distracting or even absurd. The best way to look at the subject is to think of your garden as an outdoor room and not fill it with objects like an antiques shop, but simply make yourself comfortable in it.

A POTATO FIELD TRANSFORMED

AMERICAN/ENGLISH STYLE

T his garden was created out of the thankless agricultural flatlands of eastern Long Island in the miraculous time span of five years. It was the result of meticulous planning, meticulous soil preparation, and an absolutely unshakable faith in the spirit of the place.

The garden belongs to Ngaere Macray Zohn, owner/publisher of Sagapress, familiar to garden enthusiasts for its books on horticulture and landscape history. Her profession has thus allowed her access to some of the finest garden writers of the last two centuries, such as William Robinson, Andrew Jackson Downing, Gertrude Jekyll, and Beatrix Farrand.

"I am steeped in their work," concedes Mrs.

Previous page: Through the porch of the house, one side of the garden is untamed nature— meadow and woods.

Far left: The other side of the house presents its formal face— terrace, raised beds, and lawn.

Left: From this uncompromising landscape came an English-style flower garden.

Below: The cheerfully planted terrace brings color to the house.

Zohn. "And I could not have had better teachers. A lot of what I have done is influenced by their ideas and their philosophies."

Mrs. Zohn was given *tabula rasa,* in that neither house nor garden existed on the land before 1983. "I designed the house backwards from the garden," she says, "just as the great architects like Andrew Jackson Downing used to do. I selected the site of the house based on the land, and the style of the house was dictated by the land—a kind of Long Island barn situated around a courtyard-farmyard, with a bedroom wing tacked on to the opposite side as in much old Long Island architecture. Thus the whole garden was conceived at the same time as the house—a landscape architect's ideal conditions."

The house was built in 1983–84, and the construction of the garden, including walls, soil, and pool, took place in the fall of 1984. "The regrading was a huge project," she recalls. "The original grade of the land was a steady, steep slope from the house down to the woods (a bird sanctuary)—probably a differential of fifteen feet between the house and the sanctuary." This meant the garden had to be artificially raised with massive infusions of topsoil. A lucky accident facilitated this task. "The local golf club was digging out a low spot to make a lake, so I was able to make a deal with the contractor to bring all that rich alluvial subsoil to me. Sometimes after a heavy rain I still find golf balls in my flower beds!"

GARDENS IN THE LANDSCAPE

Left: Grassy steps lead from the lower garden to the pergola and pool.

Below: A low wall and a deeply dug and generously planted perennial border—including hardy geraniums, Campanula glomerata superba, stokesia, veronica, cerastium, nigella, and alpines—lead to a pergola decorated with rubrifolia, New Dawn, Dr. Van Fleet, and Inspiration roses.

Right from the start, Ngaere Zohn had a clear vision of how the garden should look. "I find it very easy to look at the land and work from there," she explains. "It tells you what it wants. I am not imposing anything. The bottom line is to start at the horizon and work inwards." She saw meadows, woods, and lines of fields. She superimposed on her mind a photograph she found in a magazine of an English garden with woods in back, walls, trellis, flowers, an image of enclosure that pleased her greatly. "I adhere to the principle of outdoor rooms," she says. "But I could not go against the Long Island landscape."

Her solution is to blend both English formality and American wilderness by means of the house that lies between them. Standing in the center of the

house, she looks out one side through a porch to meadows, cornfields, woods—an American landscape. Turning in the other direction, she sees a terrace, low walls, borders, a pergola—the formal English look so loved by gardeners. "What gives me most pleasure is the contrast between the American side and the English side. Though," she adds, "a friend who came to visit took one look at the formal garden and said, 'That's why I've never liked Europe.' For myself, I like and have both."

The planting was done in the spring of 1985. Although she does not consider herself a plantswoman, she describes the ideas behind the planting with characteristic expertise. "If you take my philosophy of working back from the horizon, you must ask, 'Where is your eye going?' And then follow

Top: From the house the eye is drawn across the lawn to the pergola, pool, and woods.

Above: Detail of the cutting garden, with snapdragons, lilies, nicotiana, and cosmos.

that. For instance, in the early spring I have a colorful distant garden. That is because the borders are low, not yet starting to bloom, and the eye wanders over them to the pool area, where the spring color comes from rhododendrons and viburnums. Then as the borders and pergola begin to blossom, the far garden becomes dormant, and the eye is brought closer to the house by all the summer color.''

Her flowers are simple and harmonious in color —nigellas, stokesias, veronicas, geraniums, campanulas, shrub roses—plants that will withstand the fierce ocean winds and salt air of the Long Island coastal climate. Down in a protected area of the land she has a cutting garden, with annuals and bulbs— lilies, snapdragons, nicotianas, dahlias. ''I don't grow vegetables because everybody else does.''

Ngaere Zohn's design sense is unusually sure, and she was helped by the house's architect, the late Eugene Futterman, who took her garden plans and redrew them to scale and in suitable proportions. But her advice is nuts-and-bolts practical. ''Spend your money at the beginning by putting in the right drainage and plenty of good topsoil. Then everything will grow well. And remember that even if you make a very thorough plan on paper, it's never quite the same in reality as you envision. We got our final configurations for this garden by marking out the boundaries on the land itself with stakes and twine, and then walking away and looking at them.''

While she invariably wonders how to improve the garden, particularly the English part (''I'm always thinking what to move''), her goal is not to get bigger. ''I want to contain the formality and naturalize more.'' If she expands at all, it will be into the meadows and woods. For like many gardeners, she feels that a good garden must ultimately be given back to the landscape that inspired it.

Opposite: *A detail of the terrace, planted with helianthemum, aquilegia, artemisia, and nepeta.*

Above: *The cutting garden has its own little section of the landscape, protected from winds and newly planted each year with useful annuals.*

Left: *The low wall outside the front driveway of the house, hugged here by banks of honesty and daisies, reflects the low walls used inside the garden to define space.*

DECORATIVE LANDSCAPING UP A
STEEP HILLSIDE

The hillside is a south-facing bank on the edge of the North Yorkshire moors. Rising up behind it is Sleightholmedale Lodge, built in 1889 as a wedding present for the grandmother of the current owner, Rosanna James, who now lives and gardens there with her family. One could hardly imagine a more dramatic site, set in one of England's most well loved northern landscapes, with moors, streams, and wooded hillsides attracting hikers and visitors from all parts of the world.

It is said that it is difficult to design a garden when the house is in the center of the property, cutting the land, as it were, in half. It might have been particularly problematic in this case since the house was built in a long, thin, rambling strip, lying across the foot of a hill. This unusual layout has produced a subtle gradation of styles within the four-acre garden space that has evolved over 80 years. The turn-of-the-century garden, which spreads out up the hill above the house, is a rigidly formal, bravura display of geometry, while below the house, the formality gradually dissolves into a grassy, rock-and-shrub landscape that recedes gently into the sheep fields beyond.

The steep slope behind the house was planted in the 1910s by Everard Baring, military secretary to Lord Curzon, Viceroy of India. He designed it, with great originality at that time, as a rose garden, inspired by the wonderful rose gardens he had seen

when serving in India. He carved roughly one acre into four little gardens within a bigger garden, framed by oak trellises and divided by a main axial path leading up from the back of the house. The two upper gardens are rectangular, and the two lower ones circular, with stone paths between. Each circle is divided by more stone paths into quarters like a cake. In each of the eight slices of cake the designer planted 40 hybrid tea roses, with colors strictly matching, new variety next to new variety—a novelty to Victorians, but a problem today, as Mrs. James explains.

"It is difficult to grow roses in the same place for decades. The soil can't stand it. The roses get weaker and weaker. And fashions change. We don't really like hybrid teas grown like this anymore, particularly without any ground cover. They make a show from June until frost, but now we long for something else."

To change a garden as structured as this is a major task, and Mrs. James has been taking it slowly. She has taken out some of the roses and put in bulbs and flowers such as campanula, delphiniums, alchemilla, London pride, and plants that grow low, so as to allow the shape of the gardens to be seen more clearly. "I want to restore the original plan, so the lovely circular stone paths show." She is also planting according to the flowers' seasons, which means some part of the garden is constantly in bloom, and is adding vegetables to complement the flowers.

Some of the trellises are rotting with age, but to remove a trellis means removing the climbers which cling to it—in many cases, old and valuable roses. The gardener must harden her heart in such cases and quickly replace them with new planting. In some places where a new trellis has been put in, instead of roses Mrs. James has planted loganberries, blackberries, apples, redcurrants. "I like fruit-fences, particularly edging a vegetable garden."

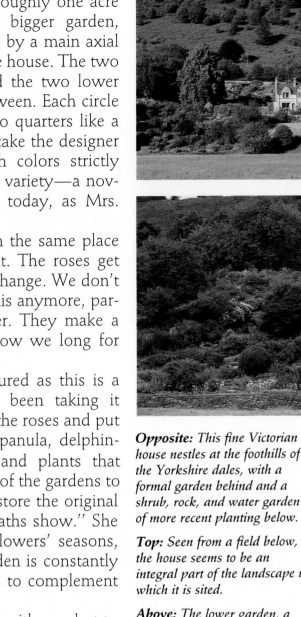

Opposite: *This fine Victorian house nestles at the foothills of the Yorkshire dales, with a formal garden behind and a shrub, rock, and water garden of more recent planting below.*

Top: *Seen from a field below, the house seems to be an integral part of the landscape in which it is sited.*

Above: *The lower garden, a lush jungle of shrubs and waterplants.*

Left and opposite: *The pond in the lower garden was made in the 1950s. Simple stone steps take one down the slope below the house and through the shrub and wildflower bank.* Primula florindae *and* potentilla *are yellow counterpoints to the lush green scenes.*

Below: *A flowering cherry tree and daffodils mark the season in this section of the informal spring garden.*

To add to the impact of the sculpted landscape rising up the hill behind the house, Mrs. James's mother, who has looked after this garden with much care for 50 years, added a second garden below the house, planting the bank with shrubs, bulbs, and rock plants, and making a small pool with water lilies at the bottom. Also below the house is a walk, consisting of an avenue of cherry trees dating from 1910, plus a spring garden added later, with azaleas and wildflowers, and a shrub walk planted with forsythia, species roses, and witch hazel. "The walks evolve and change," says Mrs. James. "But it is all very loose. We are very careful not to blot out the landscape."

It is difficult not to be aware of the landscape when walking through this garden. The magnificent circular gardens up the hill lead the eye on to the peaks of the dales above, while the original terraced front garden and stone steps below take one through a simple iron gate into the peaceful pastures beyond. And yet the formal structure sits comfortably within the wild moorland that surrounds it. "It's much easier to work with a pattern," says Mrs. James, "particularly when the pattern is organized by season rather than color, as it is here, the plan being to have different parts of the garden blooming throughout

Opposite: *A small wrought-iron gate opens onto a vista of floral abundance rising up the hill to the summer house.*

Above left: *The same view in winter—a vivid example of the architectural "bones" of an elaborately structured garden.*

Above: *One of the paths traveling from the top to the bottom of the rose-covered slope, showing the stunning contrast between designed and natural landscape.*

Above: *A wall, almost hidden by climbing roses, outlines the perimeter of the upper garden, and a path traverses its length, with perennials spilling over in enthusiasm.*

Opposite: *A high view of the ornamental rose garden, showing the circles, paths, trellises, and a dizzying display of color.*

the year. When there's a space in the garden for a plant, I know which season it should flower in and can match it to its neighbors. This greatly reduces the problem of planting a beautiful new plant, just in bud, next to one which is dying an unsightly death.''

Working with only one gardener, Mrs. James is hoping to restore the garden to its former glory—only without the hybrid teas. To help pay for this long-term project, she has converted some farm buildings into summer vacation cottages, each named after its former role, such as the Dairy, the Dovecote, the Barn, the Granary, and the Stable. Visitors staying here get to see the garden, which is also open as part of the National Gardens Scheme.

Left: *The path crossing the top of the rose garden past the summer house leads out of the garden to a small orchard.*

Above: *A simple, almost austere exit. "This garden must never blot out the landscape," says Rosanna James.*

A TINY GARDEN TUCKED INTO A
LARGE SPACE

The story of this garden could be a primer for first-time gardeners. It is very small, very simple, can be run single-handedly, and provides inexhaustible pleasure. Its inspiration, as is so often the case, came from the house, a 100-year-old Long Island farmhouse. With it came a privet hedge, a terrace, and a large expanse of flat landscape. When Pamela Lord married painter Sheridan Lord and moved into the house in 1975, "There was nothing," she says. "Certainly no mystery. It was completely flat, agricultural land with a small orchard. The potatoes came right up to the back door."

Her primary goal was to try to create some mystery. She decided on a *potager,* or ornamental vegetable garden, as being appropriate to the house. "Besides," she confesses, "I was sure I would fail. And if I failed with this garden, we could always eat it." She sited the garden behind the privet hedge, concealed from view—which was perfectly all right with Mrs. Lord. If she made mistakes, nobody could see them. "I brought with me some magnolias," she says. "And a very rare yellow-berried holly. I have always liked French gardens, with their ordered rows of vegetables, so I kept that idea in the garden, adding marigolds and colorful annuals, though I later became disenchanted with them."

The garden was designed to be seen from her husband's studio, as well as from an upstairs bedroom/office. She carved out a series of little raised

beds, four by eight or six by three feet, a size she felt she could manage on her own. She laid out several of these beds on the diagonal, the way the French do, to counteract the flat geometry of the landscape. Gradually she widened the grass paths between the beds and edged them with box, to give the garden form. In these beds she planted vegetables, cutting flowers, perennials, and again, for form, two topiary rosebushes.

"I kept some scrappy notes and made plans in my head," she remembers, "but most garden planning is about thinking. Later the plants tell you what to do. A flower you like might be happy in your brain but not in the ground." After her fling with marigolds, she decided to stick to cool colors in the garden (such as delphiniums, violas, irises, asters), and to enliven the terrace with the hot colors (coral geraniums, petunias, bright blue veronica, stella d'oro daylilies). All of these are in pots that she moves around during the summer for effect.

Through all this, Mrs. Lord remained true to the "spirit of the place," never allowing her little formal garden to stray farther into the flat lawnlike field that dominates the rest of the property and merges with the farmland beyond (the subject matter of many of her husband's paintings). The juxtaposition of the two landscapes, one so small and elegant, the other

Opposite: *Long Island architecture in its purest native form—and a gem of a garden laid out neatly in front of it.*

Above left: *Standing under the cherry tree, one looks back at the small formal pattern of beds and the "door" through the privet hedge to the patio.*

Above: *Through the privet arch the vista continues past the little front garden to the flat landscape beyond.*

Top: *Lavender, plumbago, thalictrum, salvia, sedum, perovskia, campanula—the perennial gardener's ingredients for a subtly flavored garden, with standard hollies for spice.*

Above: *Through the privet hedge, vistas of delicate color.*

Opposite: *Like a mirage, the little formal garden edges its way into the flat expanse of farmland out of which it was formed.*

stretching endlessly toward the horizon, seems almost surreal, a tiny pocket of sophistication in a rural world.

Modest gardener though she professes to be, Pamela Lord grew up gardening, both near Philadelphia with her English-born mother and on a Maryland farm with her American grandmother. With this unusually strong family tradition in her bones, it was not likely that she would keep her shrinking violet of a *potager* behind the privet hedge for long. As the garden developed, she felt confident enough to make a window in the hedge, in the manner of the European clair-voyée, so curious visitors could peek through and see her handiwork. She also attempted to start a garden on the terrace side of the hedge, but found it too demanding to keep up. Instead, the window in the hedge turned into a door, creating a charming entrance into her little French-inspired plot.

To create further interest and a shady destination at the garden's end, she planted a cherry tree and pruned it up like an umbrella, providing beneath it the perfect site for a miniature shade garden, with fragrant plants—lilies of the valley, hyacinths, fragrant lilies, a small-leafed lilac ("Miss Kim"), daphne, *Viburnum juddii*, white-flowering hosta, *Dictamnus albus*. "A great little garden for Sherry to enjoy when he sits outside listening to baseball games."

Opinionated like most gardeners, Pamela Lord does not believe that in America it is possible to have a real English-style garden. "As a child I grew up eyeball-to-eyeball with delphiniums, and it marks you. But to make them grow here I have to plant them in a protected corner and stake them very carefully. I've almost given up on roses, except for *Rosa glauca* and New Dawn, because of the dreaded Japanese beetle, but now I'm trying a few again. I also love growing woodland plants, like primula and fragrant azaleas, but we're short of shade here, the

orchard is too far away, so we must settle for the little cherry tree."

With time and practice, she feels her eye has gotten subtler, but she's not so sure that is a good thing. "I stopped planting marigolds and all that noisy stuff, but now I like it again." Perhaps surprisingly, considering her modest approach to gardening, Mrs. Lord's future dreams call for a huge conservatory with a pool in it. "I know it sounds crazy, but people in England are doing it. It would be an extravaganza, of course, a warm winter garden filled with oleanders." This fanciful dream is typical of this gardener's cheerful view. "I'm a child in the garden," she admits. "I grow plants to commemorate things—a blast of orange lilies like fireworks, for instance, for the Fourth of July. Well, why not?"

Opposite: Brilliant veronica "Crater Lake Blue" brings movable color to the Lords' terrace.

Above left: Lupines, Iris tectorum, *white hosta,* Dictamnus albus—*aromatic plants make a shade garden under a magnolia tree by the terrace.*

Above right: In one of the triangular beds, a standard holly is surrounded by perennials and evergreen powder puffs of box.

Paths, Steps, Borders, and Gates

There is not much point in making a garden if you can't walk around it, or weed it, in comfort. For practical reasons, therefore, paths and steps are essential components of garden design. There is also the element of surprise that can be obtained by the strategic use of gates and enclosures, quite apart from the wish to prevent unauthorized sightseers from admiring your handiwork.

Most of the gardeners in this book have firm views on these matters, as on every aspect of their gardens. Whether a path should be narrow or wide, curved or straight, paved or with gravel, for instance, are issues hotly debated, and their conclusions are as various as the choices. The main point seems to be that there are as many types of paths, steps, borders, and gates to define your garden as there are flowers to decorate it.

A DRAMATIC ROCK GARDEN IN
NORTHERN CALIFORNIA

There is an unprecedented revival in interest in the work of the pioneer landscape architects of this century. Gertrude Jekyll, Beatrix Farrand, and Russell Page are now almost household names to most gardeners. To these we must add Thomas D. Church, who was not so well known worldwide after his death in 1978, but who is currently emerging as one of the most important landscapists in America since H. H. Richardson and Frederick Law Olmsted. His gardens, cherished in many parts of the country, are of particular consequence in California, where he lived and worked. His ideas and dicta are worth the closest scrutiny, particularly for anyone aspiring to a garden in that testing climate.

Top: *The house and pool, seemingly an organic unit, were designed and built at the same time.*

Above left: *Pennisetun, or fountain grass, a feather-tipped grass both elegant and drought-resistant.*

Above right: *A lemon tree, breath-of-heaven, and star of jasmine reflect in natural fashion the sculptural rock forms.*

The owner of this garden knew Thomas Church because his parents had used the designer in earlier years. "I had no conception of what kind of garden I wanted," he recalls. "I just had the site." But Mr. Church, as was his custom, involved the owner in every aspect of the design, making him an active participant. "He and I drove around the nurseries in a golf cart and selected the plants. He encouraged me to be on site and made me feel I was doing it myself."

The design exhibits many of Thomas Church's trademarks. His first priority was meticulous attention to the position of the house and surrounding natural landscape. Church was known to have requested architects to change the siting of a new house in order to make the most of sun and shade. (On one occasion he turned a blueprint upside down!) This house is situated in a spectacular southern position overlooking a mountain range, and the designer has placed the garden to make the most of this natural vista, leading the eye out to a softly mounded lawn beyond the pool that seems to flow directly into the distant trees and hills. Beyond this vista, where the ground dips down the hill, a vegetable garden has been planted to take advantage of the protected southern exposure, to which, since 1971, a vineyard has been added.

The house has an Oriental flavor, and its long windows and terrace were designed to take in every aspect of the landscape outside, in the words of Mr. Church, "allowing the house and garden to become better acquainted." While it is customary in landscaping today to add foundation planting to a new house, this plan does not follow the trend. Thomas Church explains: "Too much enthusiasm in planting at the base of a house can do a garden in quicker than anything else. It is a shame to veil any house in shrubbery when the house itself is well designed. To heavily fringe such a house with foundation planting is to deny its architectural entity and to

A cascading star of jasmine softens the Oriental framework of the house.

Right: *A mayten tree* (Maytenus boaria) *and star of jasmine provide lush green walls at the perimeter of the garden.*

Overleaf: *In a series of natural-looking swirls and mounds, the garden lazily uncoils—every rock in these monolithic groupings formed not by nature but by design.*

negate the strength it gives to the garden composition. The relationship between the house and garden is maintained and emphasized by light, air, and visual space flowing freely from one to the other."

The only strictures given to Mr. Church by the owner were that the garden be low maintenance, and have "a swimming pool that didn't look like one." Thomas Church's solution was to provide a kind of giant rock garden, with no time-consuming, tender flowers, but simply shrubs, grasses, and succulents that would withstand the dry, windy climate. The pool is carved in soft curves, like an enlarged rock pool, painted black. In time the water chemicals turned it to a deep grey, harmonizing with the rocks surrounding it. "Now when people come and see it, they ask, 'Is that a pond?' "

Rocks are another of Thomas Church's most useful design tools, particularly where lawns do not thrive. In this case, 70 tons of Sonoma fieldstone boulders were his props, each placed individually by the designer, who was by that time in his 70s, in a temperature of 100 degrees. Equally careful placement of the grasses and shrubs provides a satisfactory complement to the groupings of rocks. Contrast in texture was another effect much practiced by Mr. Church. "By their shape, color, and foliage texture, plants show that they are intended to enhance architecture, not hide or compete with it," he said. He often used combinations of grass, gravel, cement, and rocks in the same area of a garden to retain moisture and add interest to edges and borders.

His shapes and patterns always had a reason. "One of the subtle things that happens in this garden is created by the shape of the lawns at the edge of the hillside," explains the owner. "He built three mounds on which to lay out the lawns that enclose the swimming pool. This gives the area an intimacy that a flat lawn would not do." The paved circle attached to the far side of the pool is no accident either. "What is the white circle?" the owner asked

him when Church showed him the plan. "That is a white circle," answered Thomas Church. "A formal shape to offset the informality of the garden."

The sculptural nature of the garden is especially apparent at night, when the boulders take on a monumental quality. The garden lights are concealed in clumps of grass, and also in trees, another favorite Church technique. Its qualities of serenity and grace, inviting the visitor to sit outside and admire the view, are achieved by careful placement of rocks and water—in artful imitation of Nature.

Opposite top: *Designer Thomas Church called this unusual upright rock The Naked Lady. "Every garden should have one," he declared.*

Opposite below: *The swordlike leaves of New Zealand flax and mats of low-lying juniper bring contrast to the smooth, sensuous boulders.*

Above: *Rocks fringed with evergreens are used as sculpture, boundaries, and furniture.*

ONE GARDEN, TWO DESIGNERS—A
STUDY IN CONTRASTS

Situated in the heart of the English Cotswolds, Abbotswood is a typical mid-19th-century country house built in the rather heavy Gothic style favored by the Victorians. Its earliest official dating comes from a charming plaque inset under a window in the front facade which says, "Lionel Charles George Sartoris, at the age of 6 years and 6 months, fell from this window, height of 18 feet 5 inches, and by God's Mercy received no injury. August 23, 1869."

The interest in the house comes from its early 20th-century additions by Sir Edwin Lutyens, whose name will live forever, apart from its place in the architectural canon, because of his association with Gertrude Jekyll. The 12 acres of grounds were

Left: *View from the bottom of the garden looking back toward the house, over a sequence of design elements—pool, steps, walls, parterre—that have their roots in the High Renaissance.*

Above: *Positioned at a window in the house, the eye takes in the formal, geometric beds and moves past the sunken pool garden and out into the pastures dotted with sheep.*

Above: The so-called Tank Garden, a Sir Edwin Lutyens addition, made of local Cotswold stone, giving a mellow appearance to the lily pond.

Right: A narrow Lutyens-designed archway leads from the front entrance of the house to the formal gardens. The fragrant pink-tipped climber on the left is Chinese gooseberry (Actinidia kolomikta).

Far right: Looking down the stream garden, a steep hillside running alongside the house, planted with acers, junipers, azaleas, spring bulbs, and other shrubs favored by Russell Page.

PRIVATE LANDSCAPES

Above: Lutyens loved gates with high columns, marking the transition from formality to pastureland.

Above right: One of the formal rose gardens, planted with hybrid teas, including Mischief, Elizabeth of Glamis, Dainty Maid, Sue Lawley, and Sylvia.

Opposite: Grassy paths meander past beds planted with spring bulbs and punctuated with tall juniper and cypress columns.

Overleaf: The formal garden dazzles with annual and perennial color, the round beds anchored by high domes of yew.

worked on both by Lutyens and by Abbotswood's owner, Mark Fenwick, himself a man of great artistic talent. It is said that Miss Jekyll visited the site, and it is hard to imagine this outspoken horticultural genius withholding her opinions of her colleague's efforts, particularly since some of the plantings at Abbotswood are quintessentially Jekyll—an old blue columbine, for instance, one of her favorites.

But equally interesting is the presence in the garden of legendary landscape architect Russell Page. In the late 1920s, when still very young and a novice at his chosen profession, Page was brought in to help Mark Fenwick, then an old man and crippled with arthritis. One can hardly do better than to quote Mr. Page himself, writing about Abbotswood in his book, *The Education of a Gardener.*

"[Mark Fenwick] had been busy making part of his hillside into a 'wild' garden where several small streams and a few outcropping stones were the excuse for a huge collection of rock and water-loving plants, alpines and flowering shrubs. Morning and afternoon, Mark Fenwick would heave himself into his electric bath-chair, see that his note-book and pencil were securely fastened to his coat by bits of string, summon Mr. Tustin his head gardener, and

off we would set. In spite of his bewildering collection of different plants, Mark Fenwick showed an extraordinary taste. His plants looked happy and he managed to arrange their placing with a delicate sense of colour and a remarkable appreciation of form and texture. I came to know this garden at every season, from the first young growth of *Cercidiphyllum japonicum* and the flowering of the tulip species, anemones and primulas in spring to the October scarlets of Japanese maples, the mauve of autumn crocuses and the muted tones of the heath garden in winter."

This passage is typically self-effacing, and yet we know that much of the planting seen today comes from Russell Page's sure eye as well as his patron's. The 12 acres of Abbotswood gardens lie on a hillside in the rolling Cotswold countryside. They are divided into different themes, originating in Lutyens's plans for a rose garden, a sunken garden, a lawn, and a tank (water) garden, while Page's additions extended up the slope at the back of the house to include a stream, a ravine, and heather and alpine gardens. Lutyens thus provided the formal, European, Victorian-style layout and Page the informal, wild, rocks-and-water landscape. Interestingly, although Page said he owed a great artistic debt to Lutyens and Jekyll, whose works were his "bible," he found Lutyens's style here "over-mannered." Certainly the later landscaping, done in Mr. Fenwick's last years, was in complete contrast to Lutyens's work, and vintage Page.

In Lutyens's time there was a pergola adjacent to the rose garden, which has since been removed. Otherwise the formal gardens remain faithful to the architect's original conception. Page's task was to install a rock-and-stream garden. He was devoted to water gardens, and his description of the Abbotswood waterworks is worth repeating.

"[The garden] lay on a hillside backed to the north by a sheltering belt of trees. From a paddock

Opposite: *Standing at the upper level of the heath garden, the visitor can see the soft mounds of variegated heathers toward the dramatically contrasting formal garden and the rolling English countryside beyond.*

Top: *The Blue Garden—forget-me-nots, pink tulips, and salvias.*

Above: *Polyanthus hybrids and* Scilla sibirica *bring a carpet of color to a weathered bench.*

Above: The Ravine Garden, Russell Page's masterpiece of trees, shrubs, rocks, and water. Spring bulbs—daffodils, anemones, scillas—and the yellow Primula florindae *add delicate color to the dramatic range of Page's acers, smoke-bushes, cypresses, and thuyas.*

Right: A typical Page mixture of wild and contrived planting.

beyond, a spring had been tapped and the water led through the wood to make three small rills. These found their way down the hillside in a series of little pools and shallow falls contrived with flattish slabs of the local yellowish limestone. The simple rock-work was unpretentious, and it looked as though the water had simply laid bare these gentle ledges apparently lying just below the surface. Patches of grass merged with the planting and the illusion of an alpine meadow was well sustained. Only when you examined the planting in detail would you discover that this was no ordinary hillside, set out as it was with gembright dwarf plants from the world's mountain ranges. An added delight in such a garden as this is the incidental music from the different notes of water as it fell from pool to pool, as characteristic in such a place as the noise of cicadas in Provence."

There you have the essence of Page's art—the naturalness, the spots of brilliant color, the trickling water, the music of the garden.

What makes Abbotswood unique, and of such interest both to the practical gardener and to the historian, is the fascinating conjunction of two great garden designers, each with totally different styles, working side by side on one large piece of land. As one drives up the long driveway to the house, the eye is irresistibly drawn toward Page's hillside, with its heavily shaded areas, watery falls, rocky resting places, and lush undergrowth. But turn toward the other side of the house, and the visitor comes upon an expansive lawn, with terraces and flights of steps so typical of Lutyens. Crossing the lawn, one is invited into the series of flower gardens that the architect designed for the main, sunken garden, and beyond it the wrought-iron gate and sheltered valleys of the Cotswolds. Thus have Edwin Lutyens and Russell Page, aided now by new patrons and a keen team of gardeners, left their powerful individual statements on the grateful landscape.

DIRECTORY

APPENDIX

FROM FARMLAND TO GARDEN IN FOUR DECADES—PLANT LIST

1. West Terrace
Cercidiphyllum japonicum, Kadsura tree
Viburnum carlesii, Korean spice viburnum
Juglans nigra, black walnut
Ulmus americana, American elm
Caragana sp., pea-tree
Ilex opaca, American holly
Picea abies, Norway spruce
Taxus sp., yew
Euonymus fortunei 'Vegetus', wintercreeper
Hibiscus syriacus, rose of Sharon
Myosotis, forget-me-not

2. Bear Garden
Buxus sempervirens, boxwood
Euonymus
Malus, espaliered apples

A GREEN AND LEAFY JUNGLE—PLANT LIST

(Chosen for shade, mostly white or green, texture, scent, shape)
Robinia pseudoacacia 'frisia'
Acer palmatum drummondii
Eucalyptus gunii
Irish yew
Juniperus procumbens
Cupressus sempervirens
Luarus nobilis
Yucca gloriosa
Trachycarpus fortuneii
Buddleia davidii
Jasmina officinale and *polyanthum*
Syringa persica alba
Philadelphus virginal
Fatsia japonica
Mahonia japonica
Phormium tenax

Cytisus battandieri, praecox and *kewensis*
Camellia japonica 'white swan'
Cordyline australis
Hellebore foetidus and *orientalis*
Ruta graveolens
Eleagnus pungens
Garrya elliptica
Euphorbia
Parthenocisus quinquefolia
Hydrangea petiolaris
Vitus henryana
Passiflora caerulea
Gunnera manicata
Arum zantedeschia aethiopica
Viburnum tomestosum

A JAPANESE THEME FOR AN EVERGREEN GARDEN —PLANT LIST

The ever-blooming perennial border
Artemisia 'Silver Mound'
Linum perenne
Stachys lanata
Nepeta Mussinii
Salvia Purpurea
Iris pallida
Geranium lancastriense
Sedum 'Ruby Glo'
Dianthus
Astilbe chinensis pumila
Heuchera 'Palace Purple'
Alchemilla mollis
Geranium 'Wargrave Pink'
Astilbe 'Peach Blossom'
Aster frikartii
Helicotrichon
Berberis
Digitalis
Campanula
Lychnis Coronarius alba
Geranium 'Johnsons Blue'
Phlox 'Bright Eyes'
Geranium platypetalum
Hosta plantaginea

Perovskia
Ilex 'Green Lustre'
Aconitum 'Bressingham Spire'
Platycodon mariesii
Ruta graveolens
Anemone japonica
Delphinium 'Connecticut Yankee'
Brunnera macriphylla
Phlox 'Mt. Fuji'
Chelome lyonii
Iris siberica
Salvia 'Indigo Spires'
Cimicifuga racemosa
Boltonia asteroides 'Snow Bank'
Filipendula venusta rubra
Miscanthus sinensis variegata
Lilum specios
Hydrangea quercifolia
Pieris japonica
Tiarella cordifolia
Viburnum caresii
Clematis ramona
Euonymus 'Manhattan'

AMIBITIOUS REPLANTING WITH A SENSE OF HISTORY—PLANT LIST

Roses in the garden (partial list)

Mme Alfred Carrière
Mme Isaac Pereire
Isphahan
La Reine Victoria
Reine des Violettes
William Lobb
Felicia
Penelope
Grüss an Aachen
Gloire de Dijon
Mermaid
Albertine
Iceberg
Rosemary Rose
Aloha
Yellow Button

Chaucer
The Miller
The Reeve
Golden Wings
Nevada
Moyesii Cantabrigiensis
Fritz Nobis
Blanche Moreau
Mme Pierre Oger
Banksia
Chinensis mutabilis
Blanc Double de Coubert
Frau Dagmar Hartopp
Rosa Mundi
Ferdinand Pichard
Fantin Latour
Wedding Day
The Garland
Rambling Rector

AUSTERE ANGLES AND VOLUPTUOUS PLANTING— PLANT LIST

Perennial borders in sunken garden
Apricot foxglove
Dicentra s. alba
Lilium regale
Rubrum, Rubrum album
Crambe cordifolia
Artemisias
Hollyhocks (singles)
Scotch Thistles
Pulmonaria
Stachys lanata
Rosa Mundi
Apothecary rose

SOURCE GUIDE

CATALOGS

There are over 400 up-to-date garden catalogs in the library of the Pennsylvania Horticulture Society. At least 50 percent of these are devoted solely to seeds. The rest include mail-order plants, garden equipment, and other horticultural items. Many gardeners grow all their plants from seed and consider it the only way to garden. Planting from seed is cheaper, easier, and in many cases, more successful. Other people, acculturated in this instant-gratification world, are too impatient for the seed to grow and prefer to buy rootstock—plants already growing above the soil. But whether you prefer to work with seeds or plants, the catalogs provide deliriously satisfying reading, particularly since they arrive in the dead of winter, when the gardener is grounded indoors and may dream his dreams unchecked.

This directory has divided seed and plant stock catalogs into separate listings. However, some houses offer both seeds and plants, which they indicate on their catalog covers. The listing is necessarily incomplete. New catalogs sprout up every year, and old ones fold or merge. There are catalogs for the most specialized of plantsmen and the most specific of geographical areas. This list names the most well known of those available at press time. Most companies ask that you send a self-addressed stamped envelope if you request a catalog.

SEED CATALOGS —U.S.

Abundant Life Seed Foundation
P.O. Box 772
Port Townsend, WA 98368
Specializes in "heirloom" seeds—seeds that date back to America's first gardens.

Botanic Garden Seed Co.
9 Wyckoff Street
Brooklyn, NY 11201
Specializing in wildflowers.

Burgess Seed & Plant Co.
905 Four Seasons Road
Bloomington, IL 61701
No-nonsense seed and plant listings.

W. Atlee Burpee & Co.
300 Park Avenue
Warminster, PA 18974
One of the largest and most famous seed houses in the U.S.

Comstock, Ferre & Co.
263 Main Street
P.O. Box 125
Wethersfield, CT 06109
Offers seeds dating from the mid 19th century.

Cook's Garden
P.O. Box 65
Londonderry, VT 05148
A huge listing of seeds for cooks.

Country Garden
Route 2
Crivitz, WI 54114
Specializes in flowers for a cutting garden.

Fragrant Path
P.O. Box 328
Fort Calhoun, NE 68023
Lists mostly seeds for fragrance.

H. G. German Seeds
201 West Main Street
Box 398
Smethport, PA 16749
One of the most expensively presented listings.

Goldsmith Seeds
P.O. Box 1349
Gilroy, CA 95021
As glossy and glamorous as a Bloomingdale's catalog.

Gurney's Seed & Nursery Co.
Second and Capital
Yankton, SD 57079
One of the major seed companies in the U.S.

Harris Seeds
961 Lyell Avenue
Rochester, NY 14606
Very extensive listing of flowers and vegetables.

Heirloom Gardens
P.O. Box 138
Guerneville, CA 95446
Specialists in heirloom seeds.

High Altitude Gardens
P.O. Box 4238
Ketchum, ID 83340
For those living at high altitudes.

J.L. Hudson, Seedsman
P:O. Box 1058
Redwood City, CA 94064
Huge listing, including a rare seeds supplement.

Jardin du Gourmet
P.O. Box 32
West Danville, VT 05873
Famous for its culinary seeds.

Johnny's Selected Seeds
Foss Hill Road
Albion, ME 04910
Caters to heirloom seed collectors.

Jung Quality Seeds
Randolph, WI 53956
Lists seeds and plants in newspaper format.

Kilgore Seed Co.
1400 West First Street
Sanford, FL 32771
Seeds for Florida gardens.

D. Landreth Seed Co.
180–188 West Ostend Street
Baltimore, MD 21230
Lists seeds available since the 1800s.

Le Marché Seeds
P.O. Box 190
Dixon, CA 95620
Culinary seeds, including those from other countries.

Letherman's
1221 East Tuscarawas Street
Canton, OH 44707
Offers a very beautiful catalog.

Maver Nursery
Route 2
Box 265B
Asheville, NC 28805
*Lists over 4,000 plants in a
computer printout.*

McLaughlin's Seeds
P.O. Box 550
Mead, WA 99021
*Specializes in wildflowers of the
Pacific Northwest.*

Nichols Garden Nursery
1190 North Pacific Highway
Albany, OR 97321
Includes a huge listing of herbs.

Park Seed Co.
P.O. Box 31
Greenwood, SC 29648
*One of the largest houses in the
U.S., offering seeds and plants.*

Pinetree Garden Seeds
Route 100
New Gloucester, ME 04260
Good prices, interesting selection.

Plants of the Southwest
1812 Second Street
Santa Fe, NM 87501
*Specializing in the Southwest
region.*

Prairie Nursery
P.O. Box 365
Westfield, WI 53964
Offers a listing of wildflowers.

Seed Savers Exchange
Route 3
Box 239
Decorah, IA 52101
Members exchange heirloom seeds

Seeds Blum
Idaho City Stage
Boise, ID 83706
*Lists unusual seeds, with essays
and recipes.*

Shepherds Garden Seeds
7389 West Zayante Road
Felton, CA 95018
*Beautifully produced catalog, listing
many European culinary seeds.*

Stokes Seeds Inc.
Box 548
Buffalo, NY 14240
Good vegetable selection.

Territorial Seed Co.
P.O. Box 27
Lorane, OR 97451
For gardeners west of the Cascades.

Thompson & Morgan
P.O. Box 1308
Jackson, NJ 08527
*The American arm of this
distinguished English house.*

Otis S. Twilley Seed Co.
P.O. Box F 65
Trevose, PA 19047
*Generous listing of vegetables suited
for each state.*

Vermont Bean Seed Co.
Garden Lane
Fair Haven, VT 05743
Major listing of culinary seeds.

PLANT CATALOGS
—U.S.

Armstrong Roses
P.O. Box 1020
6500 Bonion Road
Somis, CA 93066
Rose specialists.

Kurt Bluemel
2740 Green Lane
Baldwin, MD 21013
*Perennials, ground covers,
ornamental grasses.*

Bluestone Perennials
7211 Middle Ridge Road
Madison, OH 44057
*Huge listing at very reasonable
prices.*

Breck's
6523 North Galena Road
Peoria, IL 61632
Specializes in Dutch bulbs.

Busse Gardens
Route 2
Box 13
Cokato, MN 55321
*A new nursery with fine selection of
hostas.*

Carroll Gardens
444 East Main Street
Westminster, MD 21157
Excellent perennial listing.

Donaroma's Nursery
Box 2189H
Edgartown, MA 02539
*Specializing in perennial
wildflowers.*

Holbrook Farm
Route 2
Box 223 B
Fletcher, NC 28732
Perennials and native plants.

Jackson & Perkins Co.
Medford, OR 97501
Largest rose growers in the country.

Lamb Nurseries
E. 101 Sharp Avenue
Spokane, WA 99202
*Rock-garden plants, unusual
perennials.*

Louisiana Nursery
Route 7
Box 43
Opelousas, LA 70570
Unusual plants.

McClure and Zimmerman
1422 W. Thorndale
Chicago, IL 60660
Large selection of bulbs.

Milaegers Gardens
4838 Douglas Avenue
Racine, WI 53402
Interesting perennials.

Pickering Nurseries
670 Kingston Road
Highway #2
Pickering, Ontario LIV 1A6,
Canada
Specializes in roses.

Roses by Fred Edmunds
6235 S.W. Kahle Road
Wilsonville, OR 97070
Specializes in roses.

Roses of Yesterday and Today
802 Brown's Valley Road
Watsonville, CA 95076
Specializes in roses.

Siskiyou Rare Plant Nursery
2825 Cummings Road
Medford, OR 97501
Rock-garden and alpine plants.

Spring Hill Nurseries
P.O. Box 1714
Peoria, IL 61656
*One of the best-known plant houses
in the U.S.*

Thomasville Nurseries
P.O. Box 7
Thomasville, GA 31799
Specializes in roses.

Van Engelen Inc.
Stillbrook Farm
307 Maple Street
Litchfield, CT 06759
*Bulbs at wholesale prices and
quantities.*

**André Viette Farm and
Nursery**
Route 1
Box 16
Fishersville, VA 22939
*Large, no-nonsense catalog of
general interest.*

Wayside Gardens
Hodges, SC 29695
A well-known house with a richly illustrated catalog.

White Flower Farm
Litchfield, CT 06759
One of the oldest-established nurseries in the U.S.

SEED CATALOGS —U.K.

Allwood Brothers
Mill Nursery,
Hassocks
West Sussex BN6 9NB
One of the biggest houses in England.

John Chambers
15 Westleigh Road
Barton Seagrave
Kettering
Northants NN15 5AJ.
Good source for ornamental grasses.

Chiltern Seeds
Bortree Stile
Ulverston
Cumbria LA 12 7PB
Lists unusual seeds for flower gardens.

Samuel Dobie & Son
Upper Dee Mills
Llangollen
Clwyd LL20 8SD
Annuals, perennials, and bulbs.

Hazeldene Nursery
Dean Street
East Farleigh
Maidstone
Kent ME15 0PS
A large catalog for plants and vegetables.

Suttons Seeds
Hele Road
Torquay
South Devon TQ2 7QJ
One of the most famous seed houses in England.

Thompson & Morgan
London Road
Ipswich
Suffolk 1P2.0BA
Rivals Suttons for quantity and quality.

PLANT CATALOGS —U.K.

Jacques Amand
Clamp Hill
Stanmore
Middlesex HA7 3JS
Big listing of bulbs.

David Austin
Bowling Green Lane
Albrighton
Wolverhampton, WV7 3HB
Famous for irises, peonies, roses, hardy plants.

Peter Beales Roses
London Road
Attleborough
Norfolk NR17 1AY
Rose specialists.

Walter Blom & Son
Coombelands Nurseries
Leavesdon
Watford
Herts WD2 7BH
Bulbs of all kinds, plus annuals and perennials.

Bressingham Gardens
Diss
Norfolk 1P22 2AB
Perennials, herbs, shrubs.

Carlile's Hardy Plants
Carlile's Corner
Twyford
Reading
Berks RG10 9PU
One of the best-regarded English houses.

Beth Chatto
Elmstead Market
Colchester
Essex
All the smartest gardens use this supplier.

de Jager Nurseries
Marden
Kent TN12 9BP
Bulbs and perennials.

Hillier Nurseries
Romsey Road
Winchester
Hants SO22 5DN
Trees, shrubs, and perennials.

W.E.T. Ingwersen
Birch Farm Nursery
Gravetye
East Grinstead
West Sussex RH19 41E
Specialists in rock and alpine plants.

Michael Jefferson-Brown
Weston Hills
Spalding
Lincolnshire PE12 6DQ
Gold Medal daffodils and other bulbs.

Kelways Nurseries
Langport
Somerset TA10 9SL
Bulbs, perennials, peonies, irises.

Ken Muir
Honeypot Farm
Rectory Road
Weeley Heath
Clacton-on-Sea
Essex CO16 9BJ
Hardy perennials.

Perry's Hardy Plant Farm
Theobalds Park Road
Enfield, Middx EN2 9BG
Aquatic and bog plants.

Roses du Temps Passé
Woodlands House
Stretton
Stafford ST19 9LG
Specialists in roses.

Sunningdale Nurseries
London Road
Windlesham
Surrey GU2 6LN
Wide range of azaleas, rhododendrons, perennials.

Thompson & Morgan
London Road
Ipswich
Suffolk 1P2 0BA
One of Britain's major sources.

Unusual Plants
White Barn House
Elmstead Market
Colchester
Essex CO7 7DB
Rare species of plants.

For more information on British catalogs, consult: *Shopping by Post for Gardeners,* by Joy Montague (Exley Publications).

NURSERIES

As well as obtaining seeds and plants from catalogs, gardeners may find local nurseries a useful source, particularly in providing plants suitable for their geographical area. The number of nurseries and garden centers in both the U.S. and U.K. is enormous and constantly growing, thanks to the explosion of interest in gardening. To list them here would be an impossible task. For information about nurseries in your state or area, write to:

The American Association of Nurserymen
1250 I Street NW
Suite 500
Washington, D.C. 20005
(202) 789-2900

In the U.K., consult *The Green Pages: A Guide to the Nurseries and Garden Centres of the British Isles* (Granada Publishing).

For specific information about gardens, both the U.S. and U.K. boast excellent societies in specialized fields. For general information in the U.S., write to:

The American Horticultural Society
P.O. Box 0105
Mount Vernon, VA 22121

The Garden Club of America
598 Madison Avenue
New York, NY 10022

In the U.K., write to:

The Royal Horticultural Society
80 Vincent Square
London SW1P 2PE

GARDEN FURNITURE AND ORNAMENTS

This listing includes chairs, tables, marble, stone, and iron decorations. It is only a partial list, the selection based largely on size and accessibility.

Look for advertisements in your local newspaper and in gardening magazines for smaller, specialized companies. Telephone first to check on catalog availability.

U.S.

Barlow Tyrie Inc.
63 Great Valley Parkway
Malvern, PA 19355
(800) 451-7467 or
(215) 640-1495

British American Marketing Services Ltd.
251 Welsh Pool Road
Lionville, PA 19353
(800) 344-0259

Charleston Battery Bench Inc.
191 King Street
Charleston, SC 29401
(803) 722-3842

Chippendale Furniture
3401 5th Avenue So.
Birmingham, AL 35222
(800) 325-1253

Country Casual
17317 Germantown Road
Germantown, MD 20874-2999
(301) 540-0040

Florentine Craftsmen
46–24 28th Street
Long Island City, NY 11101
(212) 532-3926 or
(718) 937-7632

Gardener's Eden
P.O. Box 7307
San Francisco, CA 94120-7307
(415) 421-4242

International Terra Cotta Inc.
690 North Robertson Boulevard
Los Angeles, CA 90069-5088
(213) 657-3752

Kinsman Company
River Road
Dept. 441
Point Pleasant, PA 18950
(215) 297-5613

Kyoto Design
409 East Street
Healdsburn, CA 95448
(707) 433-4829

Machin Designs Inc.
652 Glenbrook Road
Stamford, CT 06906
(203) 348-3048

Peter's
1320 Route 309
Quakertown, PA 18951
(215) 536-4604

Elizabeth Schumacher
947 Longview Road
Gulph Mills, PA 19406
(215) 525-3287

Smith & Hawken
25 Corte Madera
Mill Valley, CA 94941
(415) 383-4050

Southern Statuary
3401 5th Avenue South
Birmingham, AL 35222
(205) 322-0379

Trafalgar Designs
24 Phoenixville Pike
Malvern, PA 19355
(800) 722-5439 or
(215) 640-1212

Van Klassens Garden Furniture
4619B Central Avenue Road
Knoxville, TN 37912
(615) 688-2565

The Well-Furnished Garden
5635 West Boulevard
Vancouver, BC V6M 3W7,
Canada
(604) 263-9424

Otto Wendt & Co.
417 Gentry Road
Spring, TX 77373
(713) 288-8295

Wood Classics
Route #1
Box 455-8H5
High Falls, NY 12440
(914) 687-7645

U.K.

Architectural Heritage
Taddington Manor
Taddington
Nr. Cutsdean
Cheltenham,
Gloucestershire, GL54 5RY
(038673) 414

Artech
Unit 15
Burmarsh Workshops
Marsden Street
London NW5
(01) 482-2181

Arundel Stone
62 Aldwick Road
Bognor Regis
West Sussex PO21 2PE
(0243) 829151

Barnsley House Garden Furniture
Barnsley House
Cirencester,
Glos. GL7 5NT
(0285) 74561

Chatsworth Carpenters
Estate Offices
Derbyshire Estates
Edensor
Derbyshire DE4 1PJ
(024 688) 2242

The Chelsea Gardener
Sidney Street
London SW3
(01) 352-5656

Chilstone
Sprivers Estate
Horsmonden
Kent TN12 8DR
(089 272) 3553

Classic Garden Furniture Ltd.
Audley Avenue
Newport
Shropshire TF9 2NA
(0952) 813311

Clifton Little Venice
3 Warwick Place
London W9
(01) 289-7894

Andrew Crace Designs
1A Bourne Lane
Much Hadham
Herts SG10 6ER
(027984) 2685

Crowther of Syon Lodge
Syon Lodge
Busch Corner
London Road
Isleworth
Middlesex TW7 5BH
(01) 560-7979

T. Crowther and Son
282 North End Road
Fulham
London SW6
(01) 385-1375

Christopher Gibbs Ltd.
118 New Bond Street
London W1
(01) 629-2008

Haddonstone Ltd.
The Forge House
East Haddon
Northampton NN6 8DB
(0604) 770711

Italy Direct Ltd.
Ledbury
Herefordshire HR8 2DJ
(0531) 3745

Landscape Ornament
Company
Voysey House
Barley Mow Passage
Chiswick
London W4 4PN
(01) 995-9739

London Architectural Salvage
and Supply Co.
Mark Street
London EC2A 4ER
(01) 739-0448

Minster Stone Ornaments
Station Road
Ilminster
Somerset TA19 9AS
(0460) 52277

Parterre
6 High Street
Windsor
Berkshire SL4 1LD
(0753) 851548

Renaissance Casting
19 Cranford Road
Coventry CV5 8JF
(0203) 27275

Seago
22 Pimlico Road
London SW1
(01) 730-7502

Harrison Shedlow Joinery Ltd.
Stratford St. Andrew
Saxmundham
Suffolk 1P17 1LF
(0728) 4264

Traditional Trellis Ltd.
24 Holland Park Avenue
London W11 3QU
(01) 243-1090

GARDEN
BUILDINGS

This listing includes conservatories, gazebos, pergolas,
greenhouses, bridges, and
other outdoor architectural
structures. Please check by
letter or telephone for catalog availability.

U.S.

Bow House
P.O. Box 228
Bolton, MA 01740
(617) 779-6464 or 779-2271

Dalton Gazebos
7260–68 Oakley Street
Philadelphia, PA 19111
(215) 342-9804

Machin Designs (U.S.)
557 Danbury Road (Rt. 7)
Wilton, CT 06897
(203) 834-9991

Sun Designs
P.O. Box 206
Dept. 38
Delafield, WI 53018
(414) 567-4255

U.K.

County Conservatories
P.O. Box 62
Derby Box 62
Derby DE1 1WR
(0332) 291648

Machin Designs
Ransome's Dock
Parkgate Road
London SW11 4NP
(01) 223-4383

Marston & Langinger
20 Bristol Gardens
Little Venice
London W9 2JQ
(01) 286-7643

Ollerton
Samlesbury Bottoms
Preston
Lancs PR5 0RN
(025 485) 2127

Room Outside
5 Goodwood Gardens
Goodwood
Chichester, West Sussex
PO18 0QB
(0243) 776563

Walton Conservatories
Hersham Trading Estate
Lyon Road
Walton-on-Thames
Surrey KT12 3PU
(0932) 242579

GARDENS OPEN
TO THE PUBLIC

Many gardens in North
America and Britain are open
to the public throughout the
year, and it is impossible to
mention them all. The following list is restricted to
those that have particular design interest, which means
that some famous botanical
gardens have been excluded,
and also that several of the
gardens are quite small.
Please write or telephone
first for opening times.

U.S.

Agecroft Hall
4305 Sulgrave Road
Richmond, VA
(804) 353-4241

Annapolis Royal Historic Gardens
P.O. Box 278
Annapolis Royal
Nova Scotia, BOS 1AO, Canada
(902) 532-7018

Bartram's Garden
54th Street and Lindbergh
Boulevard
Philadelphia, PA 19143
(215) 729-5281

Blithewood Gardens
Ferry Road
Bristol, RI 02809
(401) 253-2707

The Cloisters
Fort Tryon Park
New York, NY 10040
(212) 923-3700

Colonial Williamsburg
Williamsburg, VA 23185
(804) 229-1000

Duke Gardens
Somerville, NJ 08876
(201) 722-3700

Dumbarton Oaks
1703 32nd Street N.W.
Washington, DC 20007
(202) 338-8278

Four Arts Garden
Four Arts Plaza
Royal Palm Way
Palm Beach, FL 33480
(305) 655-7226

Isabella Stewart Gardner Museum
280 Fenway
Boston, MA 02115
(617) 566-1401

Ladew Topiary Gardens
3535 Jarrettsville Pike
Monkton, MD 21111
(301) 557-9570

Longue Vue
7 Bamboo Road
New Orleans, LA 70124
(504) 488-5488

Longwood Gardens
Kennett Square, PA 19348
(215) 388-6741

Morris Arboretum
9414 Meadowbrook Avenue
Philadelphia, PA 19118
(215) 247-5777

Nemours
The Nemours Foundation
P.O. Box 109
Wilmington, DE 19899
(302) 573-3333

Old Westbury Gardens
Old Westbury Road
Long Island, NY 11568
(516) 333-0048

Phipps Conservatory
Schenley Park
Pittsburgh, PA 15213
(412) 622-6914

Sonnenberg Gardens
Canandaigua, NY 14424
(716) 924-5420

Stan Hywet Hall & Gardens
714 North Portago Path
Akron, OH 44303
(216) 836-5533

Stratford Hall Plantation
Stratford, VA 22558
(804) 493-8038

Tryon Palace
613 Pollack Street
New Bern, NC 28560
(919) 638-4673

Vizcaya
3251 South Miami Avenue
Miami, FL 33129
(305) 854-6559

Winterthur
Winterthur, DE 19735
(302) 656-8591

There are also nationwide garden tours, which can be found by checking with the local garden club in your state, or by contacting the following national organizations:

New York Botanical Garden Programs—(212) 220-8747
Cooper-Hewitt Museum Programs—(212) 860-6868
Arnold Arboretum Programs —(617) 524-1718
Pennsylvania Horticultural Society Members Activities—(215) 625-8250
Chicago Botanic Garden Programs—(312) 835-5440

U.K.

The best way to visit a garden in Britain is to study the two annual "bibles," in which you will find dates, times, and places of houses and gardens open to the public throughout the year.

Historic Houses, Castles & Gardens Open to the Public
British Leisure Publications
Windsor Court
East Grinstead House
East Grinstead
West Sussex RH19 1XA
(0342) 26972

Gardens of England and Wales
The National Gardens Scheme
57 Lower Belgrave Street
London SW1W 0LR
(01) 730-0359

Other helpful publications include the following:

A Guide to English Gardens
English Tourist Board
Victoria Station
London SW1W 01R
(01) 730-3488

Collins Book of British Gardens
William Collins
8 Grafton Street
London W1
(01) 493-7070

The National Trust Handbook
36 Queen Anne's Gate
London SW1H 9AS
(01) 222-9251

Scotland's Gardens
Scotland's Gardens Scheme
31 Castle Terrace
Edinburgh EH1 2EL
(031) 229-1870

Garden Tours in the British Isles are organized by The National Trust, horticultural groups, and museums. Check issues of *The Garden,* the journal of the Royal Horticultural Society, for seasonal vacation tours.

COMMERCIAL ORGANIZATIONS

Badger Holidays
Denbigh House
Denbigh Road
Milton Keynes, Beds. MK1 1YP
(0908) 367269

Eastern National Omnibus Co.
New Writtle Street
Chelmsford, Essex CM2 0SD
(0245) 56151

Galleon World Travel Ltd.
Galleon House
52 High Street
Sevenoaks, Kent TN13 1JG
(01) 859-0111

HF Holidays Ltd.
142 Great North Way
London NW4 1EG
(01) 203-3381

Hotel St. Michaels
Gyllyngvase Beach
Seafront
Falmouth
Cornwall TR11 4NB
(0326) 312707

Ladbroke Hotels
Garden Lovers Weekends
P.O. Box 137
Watford, Herts WD1 1DN
(0923) 38877

Peak National Park Centre
Losehill Hal
Castelton
Derbyshire
(0433) 20373

Spring and Autumn Garden Holidays
Dept. EG
7 Polventon Close
Falmouth
Cornwall TR11 4AS
(0326) 314744

GARDENS IN THE BOOK OPEN TO THE PUBLIC

Since all the gardens in the book are essentially private and personal landscapes, they are not generally open to the public. But a few may be visited under certain circumstances, as described below.

U.S.

The following gardens are open from time to time for charities or garden club tours by appointment only. Please write for further information.

The Robert Dash Garden
(page 12)
Madoo
Sagaponack, NY 11962

The Hester Garden (page 110)
25 Cleveland Lane
Princeton, NJ 08540

Meadowbrook Farm (page 28)
P.O. Box 3007
Meadowbrook, PA 19046

U.K.

The following gardens are open in aid of the National Garden Scheme once or twice a year. The National Garden Scheme annual booklet, *Gardens of England and Wales,* should be consulted for dates and times.

Abbotswood (page 228)
Stow-on-the-Wold
Gloucestershire

Garsington Manor (page 94)
Garsington
Near Oxford

Sleightholmedale Lodge
(page 198)
Kirkbymoorside
York YO6 6JG
Please write to this address also for more information on the summer vacation cottages.

BIBLIOGRAPHY

There are hundreds of books on gardens and gardening, but surprisingly few that concentrate in a thorough fashion on the art of garden design. Here are some of the best.

Balston, Michael. *The Well-Furnished Garden.* New York: Simon & Schuster, and London: Michael Beazley Publishers, 1986.

Church, Thomas D. *Gardens Are for People.* New York: McGraw-Hill, 1983.

Clarke, Ethne, and George Wright. *English Topiary Gardens.* New York: Clarkson N. Potter, and London: George Weidenfeld and Nicolson, 1988.

Douglas, Frey, Johnson, Littlefield, eds. *Garden Design.* New York: Simon & Schuster, 1984.

Hicks, David. *Garden Design.* London and Boston: Routledge & Kegan Paul, 1982.

Hobhouse, Penelope. *Garden Style.* Boston: Little, Brown, and London: Windward/ Frances Lincoln, 1988.

Jekyll, Gertrude. *Colour Schemes for the Flower Garden.* London: Century Hutchinson, and New York: Salem House, 1987.

Jekyll, Gertrude, and Lawrence Weaver. *Gardens for Small Country Houses.* Ithaca, NY: Antique Collectors' Club, 1981.

Kassler, Elizabeth B. *Modern Gardens and the Landscape.* New York: The Museum of Modern Art, 1984.

Keen, Mary. *The Garden Border Book.* London: Viking, and Deer Park, WI: Capability's, 1987.

Llewellyn, Roddy. *Beautiful Backyards.* London: Ward Lock, and New York: Salem House, 1985.

Page, Russell. *The Education of a Gardener.* New York and London: Penguin, 1985.

Paul, Anthony, and Yvonne Rees. *The Garden Design Book.* New York and Boston: Salem House, 1988.

Robinson, William. *The Wild Garden.* London: Century Hutchinson, and New York: David & Charles, Sterling Publishing Co., Inc.

Strong, Roy. *Creating Small Gardens.* London: Conran Octopus, 1986, and New York: Villard Books, 1987.

Turner, Tom. *English Garden Design.* Ithaca, NY: Antique Collectors' Club, 1986.

Verey, Rosemary. *Classic Garden Design.* London: Viking, and New York: Congdon & Weed, 1984.

INDEX

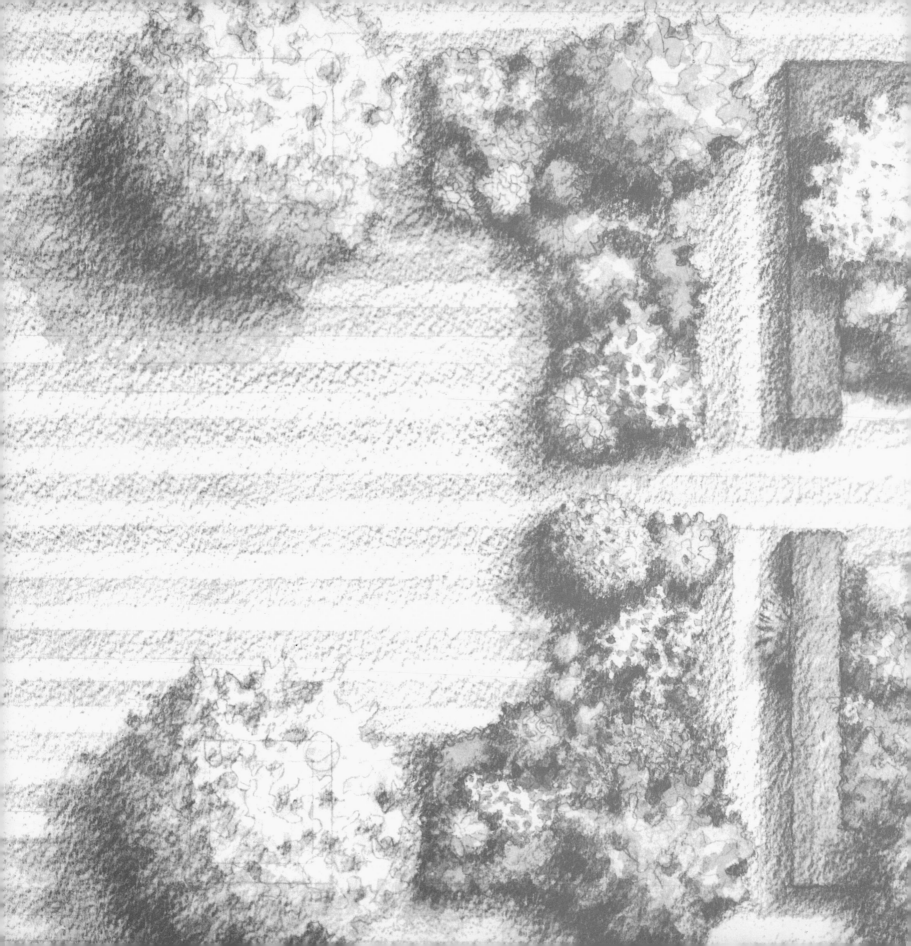